Sustainable Banking

Rosella Carè

Sustainable Banking

Issues and Challenges

Rosella Carè
DSGSES
University Magna Graecia of Catanzaro
Catanzaro, Italy

ISBN 978-3-319-73388-3   ISBN 978-3-319-73389-0   (eBook)
https://doi.org/10.1007/978-3-319-73389-0

Library of Congress Control Number: 2018932364

Cover credit: Détail de la Tour Eiffel © nemesis2207/Fotolia.co.uk

Printed on acid-free paper

This Palgrave Pivot imprint is published by Springer Nature
The registered company is Springer International Publishing AG
The registered company address is: Gewerbestrasse 11, 6330 Cham, Switzerland

FOREWORD

In the face of humanity's unsustainable journey, current geopolitical crises, and climate challenges, the implementation of the 17 sustainable development goals (SDGs) of the United Nations (UN) and the Paris climate accord (COP21) has become an unavoidable obligation for the business and investment and banking communities. Yet, scientists, investors, entrepreneurs, businesspeople, politicians, economists, civil society, and political leaders are daunted by the task at hand, and so are financial intermediaries.

In recent years, discussions of the relationship between business and society have made immense progress. The underlying intention of this work is to contribute to the world's most challenging problems by creating value for both business and society through financial intermediation. Previous volumes have considered global and professional perspectives on corporate social responsibility (CSR). Here, we focus specifically on banking, which is now in the eye of the storm.

There is no doubt about what prompted this book: the international financial and economic crisis of 2008 and ongoing research on how banks can contribute to societal welfare, to FOP 21, and to the UN SDGs. This book is novel in analyzing the concept of sustainable banking via a twofold approach (theoretical and practical) to provide a comprehensive overview of prerequisites of sustainable banking, with a focus on literature and practices. By engaging in this publishing project, Rosella is laying foundations for a future that is sustainable, ethical, and supported by sound governance. There could indeed be such a thing as "sustainable banking", allowing banks and intermediaries to be part of the solution rather than constituting the problem.

The book, as a suitable guide, should be recommended reading for all bankers and for all who are preparing for careers in financial services. All financial service professionals should be required to reflect on the issues and cases presented, and to respond in writing on their own practices against such a backdrop. There is a case for organizing dialogue seminars at universities that involve financial services professionals in countries such as the United Kingdom, Sweden, and Norway. General readers must be able to gain insights into current debates and to move on from simple stereotypes.

Sustainable banking can be viewed as a fast-growing international field that supports vital international professional debates addressing problems related to knowledge, culture, and communication.

Green bonds, social impact bonds, impact investing, and social entrepreneurship constitute good examples of sustainable finance and intermediation. First, however, one must get the foundation correct. Otherwise, the new wedding cake will crack and collapse. The foundation is the inner attitudes of investors, managers, entrepreneurs, intermediaries, and investees, as well as the integral approach to investment and finance, which includes internal and cultural dimensions of humanity.

I herewith congratulate Rosella for her achievements. I am certain that the book will make major contributions to the field of *sustainable banking*.

Funder of ECCOS Impact GmbH &   Karen Wendt
External Lecturer at Modul University (Vienna)

Acknowledgments

Special thanks to the many people who made significant contributions to my entire academic career through their technical expertise, valuable contributions, and kind support.

First and foremost, I would like to express my gratitude to my supervisor Professor Annarita Trotta for having guided me during these intense years of research. She introduced me to the studies of banking and finance, and constantly encouraged my interest in these areas.

I feel particularly grateful to Professor Olaf Weber (Waterloo University, Canada) for the many fruitful discussions we have had and for offering me the opportunity to join the Waterloo University as visiting researcher in November 2016.

During the course of my PhD studies, I was granted the opportunity to study at the Conservatoire National des Arts et Métiers of Paris (CNAM) and at the ESCP Europe of Paris. For these exceptional experiences, I have to thank Professor Yuri Biondi (University Paris Dauphine); he was not only a supervisor but also a true friend.

I am deeply thankful to Professor Patrick Boisselier (Conservatoire National des Arts et Métiers of Paris), who agreed to supervise my doctoral studies, and to Professor Dominique Torre (University of Nice Sophia Antipolis—CNRS), who was the chair of my PhD committee and a precious source of advice throughout my research activities.

I fervently thank Karen Wendt for her kind preface to this book and for her support in my research projects during the last months.

Many thanks also to Intesa Sanpaolo for contributing to Chap. 6, and in particular to Dr. Elena Flor (head of Corporate Social Responsibility),

Dr. Fabrizio Paschina (head of Advertising and Web), and Dr. Cristina Laura Paltrinieri (External Relation Department—Research & Survey).

My gratitude extends to the two anonymous reviewers who approved this book for publication.

Last but not least, I would like to thank the most important people in my life. Thank you to my sister, Stella; my best friend, Enza; and my little niece, Francesca, for having encouraged me and for their understanding and patience. They have been my anchor during storms, my great supporters, and special friends.

Finally, I take full responsibility for any flaws or errors in and any omissions from this book.

CONTENTS

List of Figures

LIST OF TABLES

CHAPTER 1

Overview

Abstract This chapter provides an overview of the structure of the book, identifying the main themes of any chapters and clarifying the main aims.

Keywords Sustainable banking • Financial crisis • Sustainable development

1.1 INTRODUCTION

The consequences of the financial crisis have strengthened interest in sustainable business models, and investors are giving increasing notice to sustainable business management that takes environmental, social, and governance (ESG) criteria into consideration. In recent times, the concept of sustainability has grown in recognition and importance, and has become one of the most talked about topics. Exponential population growth, global warming, and a growing disparity of incomes have all given rise to evermore insistent calls for social justice and environmentally friendly development.

The linkages between finance and sustainable development have been explored by many academics, and recent studies underline that sustainability can be useful in improving the stability of the financial system (Liu 2012; Alexander 2014) and that sustainability and ethical values can play a key role in finance (Lehner 2016). Being capital providers, banks can help address new economic realities linked to environmental and social (E&S) sustainability and can contribute to national sustainable development agendas (IFC 2017).

© The Author(s) 2018
R. Carè, *Sustainable Banking*,
https://doi.org/10.1007/978-3-319-73389-0_1

1

Sustainable behaviors are gradually becoming more embedded into banking business models and strategies. This signals a radical change of direction in the way that banking industry has approached financial markets in the past. Therefore, this promising approach can be considered as strategic in its intent and purposes, as banks are capable of being "sustainable" while pursuing their profit-making activities. This transformation implies that the banks' commitment may represent a viable way to add value to the business itself while also adding value to society by promoting sustainable development. Banks are currently involved in national and international sustainability programs, are included in national and international sustainability indices (e.g., Dow Jones Sustainability Index and Financial Times Stock Exchange4Good [FTSE4GOOD]), and participate in national and international business sustainability programs, such as those hosted by the United Nations. The connections between the issue of sustainable development and banking activities can be detected in the 1990s, when banks had increasingly begun to incorporate environmental requirements into their lending decisions, developed risk assessment procedures to offset potential liability for environmental damage caused by their borrowers, and developed many corporate social responsibility and risks agendas (Coulson and O'Sullivan 2013). Banks are becoming aware that their clients' mismanagement of environmental risks may affect their own business as lenders and their reputational capital (Jeucken 2011; Bouma et al. 2017). Environmental risks influence the counterparty risk; therefore, banks affect sustainable development directly—through their "day-to-day" operational activities (Case 1999; Jeucken 2011)—and indirectly, through the products and services they offer (Thompson 1998; Case 1999; Weber 2012; Bouma et al. 2017).

Actually, several key changes are occurring in the regulation and supervision of banking (and financial) systems at the international level. However, regardless of regulatory regime, several banks have incentives to voluntarily provide information regarding their engagement in sustainable practices (Carnevale and Mazzuca 2014; Carè 2017). What emerges from these conditions is that the way in which banks operate is changing. External and internal pressures are transforming the approach of banking, and in this scenario, banks can gain advantages from the new business opportunities that sustainability offers.

This book provides an exploratory analysis into the field of sustainable banking and is based on the following research objectives: (1) to explore the concept of sustainable banking both in theory and in practice, (2) to understand what the main drivers are that are pushing banks toward a more sustainable business approach, and (3) to determine the main opportunities and challenges that can be derived from this new banking concept.

In pursuing these objectives, this book utilizes the two most important definitions of sustainable banking. In particular, Weber (2012) explains that sustainable banking integrates ESG criteria into traditional banking and sets ESG benefits as a key objective. The authors also summarize the main aspects of sustainable banking as follows: (2) internal environmental management; (2) environmental credit risk management; (3) socially responsible investment; (4) carbon finance; and (5) impact investment.

The second definition is provided by Bouma et al. (2017) and highlights that "sustainable banking" can be considered a *dynamic term* because its definition changes over time and considered a term without clear borders because the relationship between banks and their stakeholders make the concept relevant to actors other than just the banks themselves. The authors also highlight a series of themes that are fairly central and interrelated, such as (1) the policies of banks, (2) communication and transparency, (3) environmental investments and environmental risks, and (4) the role of governments, nongovernmental organizations (NGOs), and multilateral banks (Bouma et al. 2017).

This book is founded upon four major aspects that characterize sustainable banking: risks, products and services, transparency and communication, and external pressures. Overall, the book is organized as depicted in the framework of Fig. 1.1.

In Fig. 1.1, the four aspects shown (transparency and communication, products and services, risks, and external pressures) are the starting point of the entire book and are analyzed both in theory through Chaps. 3 and 4 (on the left side) and in practice through Chaps. 5 and 6 (on the right side). Moreover, to address the main theme of this book, the relationship between ethics and finance has been analyzed by providing some useful insight for the understanding of the main drivers that are moving academia in considering new alternative finance and business practices. Finally, Chap. 7 draws on the previous findings of the entire book and highlights future research directions. In the following, Chaps. 2, 3, 4, 5, 6 and 7 are illustrated in more detail, and the core idea of each chapter is outlined.

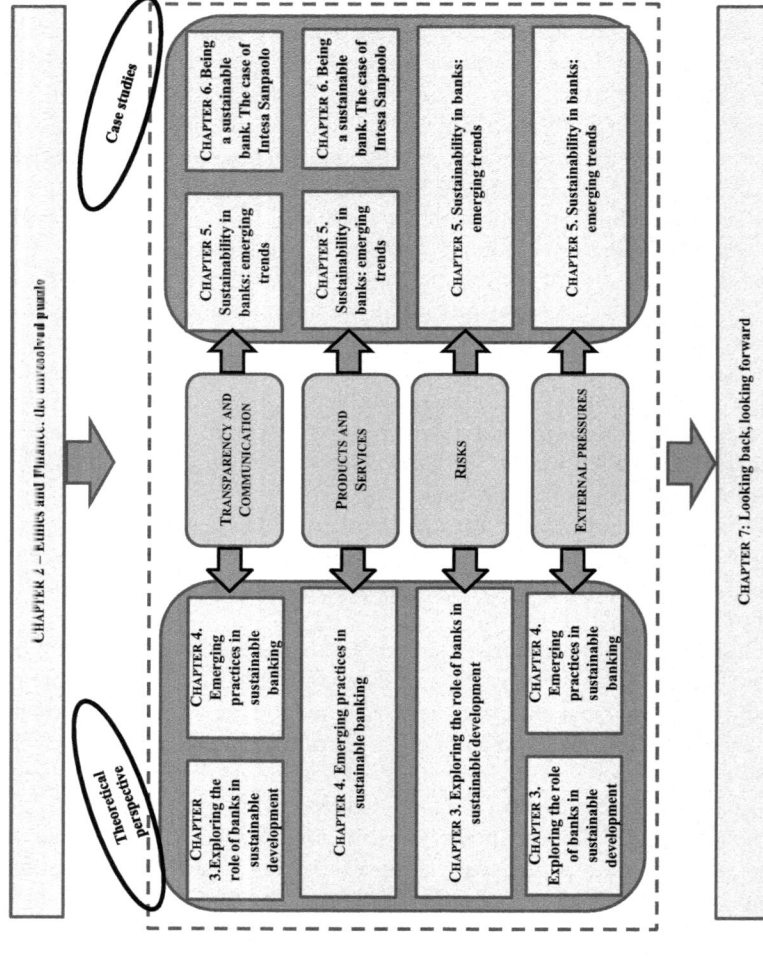

Fig. 1.1 Book outline (Source: our elaboration)

1.2   CHAPTER 2: ETHICS AND FINANCE: THE UNRESOLVED PUZZLE

The chapter moves from recent critiques of mainstream finance and provides an excursus on the role of ethics in finance. By underlining how several scholars have questioned the essence of neoclassical approaches based on rational behaviors and profit maximization, this chapter focuses on the emerging role of alternative approaches and on the themes of social finance and social banking. At the same time, the chapter outlines the new pathway that is affirming academic finance and banking research by focusing on social finance and social banking. Finally, it offers in Appendix 2.1 an analysis of two of the most important social banks and lays the basis for the comparison with sustainable banking in Chap. 7.

1.3   CHAPTER 3: EXPLORING THE ROLE OF BANKS IN SUSTAINABLE DEVELOPMENT

This chapter provides an overview of the role that banks can play in sustainable development and of the major challenges and opportunities that emerge from this new business approach. Environmental and social pressures are linked with sustainability and are the main thread of the entire book. This chapter highlights the contributions of the banking system in the achievement of sustainable development, by underlying the major changes that occurred at the international level. Then, it introduces the role of CSR practices towards sustainability in banking by focusing on the role of the credit risk management process and describes how sustainability issues might create value for banks.

1.4   CHAPTER 4: EMERGING PRACTICES IN SUSTAINABLE BANKING

Environmental concerns are pushing banks towards the development of new products and investment and communication strategies. From the banks' point of view, sustainable products may be seen as both a strategic and commercial opportunity. At the same time, communicating bank engagement in sustainable approaches may represent a pathway towards new market opportunities in terms of reputation and customer perception.

This chapter gives an overview of the most important sustainable products and services developed by the banking industry and describes the role of sustainability disclosure in terms of both opportunities and risks of inactions.

At the same time, communicating bank engagement in sustainable approaches may represent a pathway toward new market opportunities in terms of reputation and customer perception. This chapter gives an overview of the most important sustainable products and services developed by the banking industry and describes the role of sustainability disclosure in terms of both opportunities and risks of inactions.

1.5   CHAPTER 5: SUSTAINABILITY IN BANKS: EMERGING TRENDS

The chapter compares the sustainability and environmental disclosure practices of European banks from a practical point of view. Through an exploratory analysis based on multiple case studies, six banks enclosed in the Global 100 Sustainable Companies have been scrutinized. The chapter represents the starting point from which this book tries to understand what it means to be a sustainable bank from a practical perspective. In particular, it is based on the analysis of disclosed information and thus analyzes banks' behaviors and efforts towards sustainability from an external standpoint.

1.6   CHAPTER 6: BEING A SUSTAINABLE BANK: THE CASE OF INTESA SANPAOLO

This chapter—by using a single case study approach—is based on the experience of Intesa Sanpaolo Group. This chapter has been written in collaboration with Intesa Sanpaolo's External Relations Department and highlights in a comprehensive manner the bank's approach to sustainability (including its social and environmental efforts for the community). The chapter tries to analyze what it means to be a sustainable bank from an internal standpoint.

1.7   Chapter 7: Looking Back, Looking Forward

This chapter draws from the previous theoretical and empirical findings by providing an integrated framework for the comprehension of the sustainable banking phenomenon. Finally, the chapter offers suggestions and future research directions.

1.8   Methodology

This book has used a variety of methods to provide a wide overview of theoretical and practical perspectives on sustainable banking. These methods span from systematic literature review to case studies. The first three chapters are based on a theoretical analysis of sustainable banking. The book supplements this theoretical overview with practical case studies to provide readers with examples of sustainable banking activities.

Chapters 5 and 6 are based on up-to-date data and information retrieved from international databases (such as ORBIS) or from public-domain documents that can be freely accessed from banks' websites. Multiple case studies are presented in Chap. 5, while a single case study is analyzed in Chap. 6. Chapter 6 has been directly drawn up by Intesa Sanpaolo with the aim to describe—from the Bank's perspective—what they intend for sustainable banking.

1.9   Who Should Read This Book?

This book aims to provide business students, practitioners, and scholars with a broad analysis—both theoretical and practical—of what it means to be a sustainable bank. E&S pressures are the link with sustainability and the *leitmotiv* of the entire book that is organized into seven chapters, of which two are dedicated to practical case studies and analysis.

The innovativeness of this book concerns the idea of analyzing the concept of sustainable banking by using a twofold approach (both theoretical and practical), and is able to provide a comprehensive overview of sustainable banking literature and practices. The book features the following:

- Up-to-date academic literature and practitioners' points of view on the topic of sustainable banking,
- a broad outline on new sustainable banking models and strategies that incorporate E&S issues, and
- case studies focusing on the sustainable approach of banks, including deeper analyses of their disclosure activities.

This book is intended to reach an audience of both academics and practitioners. However, embracing this vision brings with it a set of challenges inherent in reaching out to such a broad audience. The importance of the topic makes this goal a necessity, even though the realms of academia and practice historically have been worlds apart. Drawing these two domains together has enormous potential for advancing the field of sustainable banking. Finally, the other potential readers of this book are business students interested in finance and banking.

References

Alexander, K. (2014). *Stability and sustainability in banking reform: Are environmental risks missing in Basel III*. Cambridge/Geneva: CISL & UNEPFI.

Bouma, J. J., Jeucken, M., & Klinkers, L. (Eds.). (2017). *Sustainable banking: The greening of finance*. New York: Routledge.

Carè, R. (2017). Exploring environmental disclosure in banks. Evidence from the Euro area. *ACRN Oxford Journal of Finance and Risk Perspectives, 6*(2), 18–40.

Carnevale, C., & Mazzuca, M. (2014). Sustainability report and bank valuation: Evidence from European stock markets. *Business Ethics: A European Review, 23*(1), 69–90.

Case, P. (1999). *Environmental risk management and corporate lending: A global perspective*. Cambridge: Woodhead Publishing.

Coulson, A., & O'Sullivan, N. (2013). Environmental and social assessment in finance. In J. Bebbington, J. Unerman, & B. O'Dwyer (Eds.), *Sustainability accounting and accountability*. New York: Routledge.

International Finance Corporation. (2017). *Sustainable banking policies, guidelines and principles*. Retrieved from http://www.ifc.org/wps/wcm/connect/topics_ext_content/ifc_external_corporate_site/sustainability-at-ifc/company-resources/sustainable-finance/sbn

Jeucken, M. (2011). *Sustainable finance and banking: The financial sector and the future of the planet*. London: Routledge.

Lehner, O. M. (Ed.). (2016). *Routledge handbook of social and sustainable finance*. London: Routledge.

Liu, S. (2012). Improving financial stability: Can European Union member states learn from China's experience in enhancing commercial banks' social responsibilities? *European Law Journal, 18*(1), 108–121.

Thompson, P. (1998). Assessing the environmental risk exposure of UK banks. *International Journal of Bank Marketing, 16*(3), 129–139.

Weber, O. (2012). Environmental credit risk management in banks and financial service institutions. *Business Strategy and the Environment, 21*(4), 248–263.

CHAPTER 2

Ethics and Finance: The Unresolved Puzzle

Abstract This chapter moves from recent critiques of mainstream finance and provides an excursus on the role of ethics in finance. By underlining how several scholars have questioned the essence of neoclassical approaches based on rational behaviors and profit maximization, the chapter focuses on the emerging role of alternative approaches and on the themes of social finance and social banking.

Keywords Mainstream finance • Ethics • Social finance • Social banking

2.1 INTRODUCTION

The global financial crisis illustrated that the expansion of the financial sector, the phenomenal sophistication of financial products, and the unprecedented velocity of financial transactions have together profoundly altered the relationships between finance, the economy, and society (Lagoarde-Segot 2017, p. 113).[1] Three main facets of the international financial system—under the ideological conditions of neoliberalism—led to the crisis: social irresponsibility, intransparency, and unsustainability (Benedikter 2011).

Irresponsibility, morally dubious behavior, and financial misconduct have had a disruptive impact on society. The emerging fields of social finance and social and sustainable banking represent attempts to include broader considerations of fairness, social values, and social justice in financial market operations.

This chapter provides an excursus on the role of ethics in finance. By showing how several scholars have questioned the essence of neoclassical approaches based on rational behaviors and profit maximization, the chapter focuses on the emerging role of alternative approaches and on themes of social finance and social banking. Finally, the appendix provides an overview of the two most important social banks to describe their main characteristics.

2.2   Concepts of Ethics Applied to Finance

The concept of ethics—and especially of a lack of ethics in business behaviors—has been brought to the fore by the crisis (Dembinski 2009; Lewis et al. 2010; Van Hoom 2015) and is considered to be an important future challenge (McCosh 1999; Stückelberger 2012). Although finance raises many ethical issues, the academic study of ethics has received little attention from scholars in the finance and business disciplines (Boatright 2010). Boatright (2010 p. 3) clarifies this issue: "*The neglect by finance scholars is understandable given the research paradigm in the field, which not only excludes normative questions from study but also demands the use of particular analytical tools and methodologies. For most finance scholars, the task of addressing ethical issues is simply not what they are trained to do.*" The ways of thinking in finance owe much to the general field of economics. Thus, finance scholars have developed the general economic conceptual framework to assume a distinctive finance-oriented view of the world (Kolb 2010).

San-Jose and Retolaza (2017) argue that the debate about ethics and finance is still open and that scholars are divided between those who consider this relationship to be an oxymoron and those who consider principles and values to be the basis of finance. In the first case, the relationship between ethics and finance is considered an oxymoron because the financial market structure leads to the maximization of profit grounded in self-interest (Dobson 1997; Werhane and Freeman 1999; San-Jose and Retolaza 2017). In this vein, Dobson (1997) highlights how something has gone wrong in the transition from the "self-interest" approach used by Smith and Hume to the "self-interest" approach used in the finance paradigm, and that traditional finance is based on rational agents that are individualistic, materialistic, and competitive (Dobson 1997). The view of business as "*amoral*" and thus the need for a separate discourse of "ethics" is described by Freeman (1994) and Werhane and Freeman (1999) via the "separation thesis" that pervades business ethics. The separation thesis is based on the following idea: "*the discourse of business and the discourse of ethics can be separated so that sentences like, 'x is a business decision' have no moral content, and 'x is a moral decision' have no business content"* (Freeman 1994, p. 5). Freeman offers a provocative explanation, clarified by Wicks (1996), for why the normative core of business research is perceived as fundamentally at odds with the pervasive wisdom on business and with the academic literature on management, while Sandberg (2008, p. 230) defines values as *"embedded in social contexts from which they cannot be removed"*.

It seems clear that one of the main critiques of mainstream neoclassical theory is that it has failed to incorporate into its corpus notions of altruism, morality, and ethics; that economic agents are completely self-interested in terms of their underlying motivational structures (Altman 2005); and that opportunism is built into financial economics in a most fundamental way (Dobson 2010).

In this vein, academics argue that contemporary economic theory is flawed (Etzioni 1988) or in need of revision (Altman 2004; Henrich 2004; Kahneman et al. 1986a, b), while others consider financial economics to be incompletely detached from ethics and value (Dobson 1991). From a theoretical point of view, Kolb (2010) identifies two more recent developments that have also involved ethical issues and, namely, issues of enterprise or integrated risk management and behavioral finance. In particular, behavioral finance developments are the result of advances in psychology that yield a more realistic understanding of people's actual financial decisions. The result has been to replace the simple view of *homo economicus* as a perfect utility maximizer with a more complex conceptualization that managers must consider in their efforts to increase firm value (Kolb 2010). Oberlechner (2007) provides an extensive review of psychological research relevant to the ethical decision-making process, while Prentice (2007, p. 17) highlights that *"the flourishing field of behavioral finance indicates that people often do not engage in optimal decision making when investing. The same cognitive biases and mental heuristics that cause suboptimal investing may also cause people to make unethical decisions. For that reason, good intentions are necessary, but they are not sufficient for finance professionals who desire to act ethically"*.

2.3   CRITICS OF MAINSTREAM FINANCE

The recent financial, economic, and social turmoil calls for a profound reconsideration of finance theory (Lagoarde-Segot 2010; Porter and Kramer 2011; Rappaport and Bogle 2011; Bay and Schinkus 2012; Shiller 2013; Krugman 2014; Lagoarde-Segot 2014; Lagoarde-Segot 2016) by questioning the assumptions and paradigms of mainstream literature

(Paranque and Pérez 2016; Lagoarde-Segot 2017; Lagoarde-Segot and Paranque 2017). One of the most interesting effects of this particular market crash is that finance theory has been directly blamed for the crisis (Fabozzi et al. 2014; Zingales 2015; Carè et al. 2018). Specifically, standard models are being questioned because they do not take into account the whole picture and especially neglect the behavioral and "human" aspects of the markets (Colander et al. 2009; Jorion 2009; Lawson 2009; Kirman 2010; Vasile et al. 2011).

The origins of modern finance are generally dated to the development of modern portfolio theory (MPT) in the 1950s and its dominant perspective is the efficient market hypothesis (EMH)[2] (Preda 2017). Mainstream academic finance is based on the following theories: (1) efficient market theory, (2) portfolio theory, (3) capital asset pricing theory, (4) option pricing theory, (5) agency theory, (6) arbitrage pricing theory, (7) capital budgeting policy, (8) capital structure policy, and (9) dividend policy (Smith and Clifford 1990; Bettner et al. 1994). Bettner et al. (1994) note that the common threads across theories and policies of mainstream academic finance include the following:

1. An underlying cause and effect mechanism animates all financial activity, and connections exist between initial conditions and final outcomes.
2. Connections are determinable, and then outcomes can be predicted with certainty.
3. All relevant human behavior is governed by the cause and effect mechanism.
4. All financial activity can be quantified, and the logic of statistical analysis and inference applies to all measurements.
5. All human beings have equal access to the institutions and systems within which financial activity is undertaken (p. 3).

The concepts of rationality and efficiency are central to contemporary economics and finance, and scholars take individuals' choices as a starting point in their analyses (Hsieh 2010).

Critiques of mainstream finance can be analyzed based on three perspectives: individual behaviors, the analysis level, and the overall conceptual framework (Paranque and Pérez 2016).

According to the individual behavior perspective, the main critiques of mainstream finance are based on the fact that it does not consider "human aspects" that may foster fear and greed (Shefrin and Statman 2000) and immoral and inappropriate behavior among financial market agents (including supporting entities, such as rating agencies and regulatory institutions) (Szyszka 2011). In this sense, classical examples of various deviations from "rationality" have been revealed by behavioral research since the 1970s. In the last 40 years, behavioral researchers have won Nobel Prizes and accumulated evidence that renders it difficult to deny that these theories challenging the underlying assumption that agents are fully rational represent a credible alternative paradigm (Gippel 2013).

Finance theory has also been criticized for the weak design of its theories (Paranque and Pérez 2016). Findlay and Williams (1985) provide a cogent critique of mainstream finance theory by arguing that its assumptions are manifestly contradicted by observations and that the capabilities of a theory to explain depend upon the methodological approaches it adopts. In the same vein, Blommestein (2009) states, "*Testing an economic theory in quantitative form requires the introduction of all sorts of ad hoc statistical or econometric modeling assumptions in order to arrive at a fully specified empirical model. This ad hoc nature of economic model building generates a significant degree of specification uncertainty. [...] Semantically insufficient theories, therefore, make it very hard to formulate reliable empirical models. In other words, the big problem with economic theories is not that they are too simplistic or that so-called 'unrealistic' assumptions are being used, but it is their semantical insufficiency (low degree of testability)*" (p. 71). To describe how "mainstream finance" maintains its hegemony, Keasey and Hudson (2007) bring to light that "*researchers take data from the outside world, often ignoring the rich complexities of the context which has given rise to the data, and creates puzzles where the data does not fit into the traditional core of the subject. These puzzles then act as catalysts for research activity as researchers try to 'solve' them. As a description of this research process we use the metaphor of 'A House Without Windows'*" (p. 933). In the metaphor used by Keasey and Hudson (2007), the community of finance scholars lives inside the house and their debates and models are internally consistent, but they require "new facts" if the debate is to be kept alive. However, rather than attempting to view the actions of individuals firsthand or to engage in debates with individuals who are involved in financial decision-making, the finance community prefers to stay safe and to use data from the world outside. The problem is that these data feeds are interpreted from their shared paradigms. In this way, anomalies give rise to new debates that attempt to reconcile them with the existing paradigm (Keasey and Hudson 2007).

2.4   From Critics of Mainstream Finance to Social Finance and Social Banking: A New Humanistic Approach

The 2007/2009 financial crisis has shaken investors' confidence in established market ideologies by renewing interest in the impacts that investments may have and by renewing interests in what could be considered "alternative finance". As noted by Shiller (2013, p. 10), finance should be defined not merely as the manipulation of money or as the management of risk but also as the stewardship of society's assets. The author argues for the need to envision new ways to rechannel financial creativity to benefit society as a whole. Indeed, this shift toward social finance can, in its essence, be considered part of a basic mind-set shift under the influence of the crisis, one that highlights a new "financial humanism" taking the form of a heightened responsibility for sustainable development in the social and environmental spheres (Benedikter 2011).

In the academic literature, social finance can be considered a relatively new development in the international banking and finance sector (Benedikter 2011; Hangl 2014; Joy et al. 2011; Lehner and Nicholls 2014).[3] According to the conceptual approach applied by Weber (2012, p. 3), social finance is "an umbrella term for financial products and services that strive to achieve a positive social, environmental or sustainability impact". Moore et al. (2012, p. 116) note that "social finance refers to the deployment of financial resources primarily for social and environmental returns, as well as in some cases, a financial return".

Social finance is based on a set of values that gives priority to ethical and ecological choices, social utility, public interest, local development, and long-term returns over short-term profit maximization (Vandemeulebroucke et al. 2010). In particular, Nicholls and Pharoah (2007, p. 2) underline that it refers to more than just the flow of money into social or environmental projects, as it is conceived as an ethos of the way money is used. A deeper understanding of social finance has not been facilitated by the numerous terms applied to the concept of intentional investing for positive social impact (Harji and Hebb 2010). Social finance, social investment, and impact investment are commonly used as synonyms (Moore et al. 2012). Höchstädter and Scheck (2015) stress that social finance and social investment are not perfectly congruent with impact investing. Instead, these authors consider impact investing to be a subtype of social finance/investment (Höchstädter and Scheck 2015). As the main distinction between conventional and social finance, the latter uses financial services and products to achieve a positive impact on society, the environment, or sustainable development (Weber 2012; Weber and Duan 2012). Social finance can be generally classified into three main categories: (1) social banking, (2) impact investing, and (3) microfinance (Weber and Duan 2012). Social banking is conducted by social, ethical, or alternative banks and partly by cooperative banks and credit unions (Weber and Remer 2011). In contrast to conventional banks, social banks provide loans to create a social or environmental benefit (Edery 2006; da Silva 2007). Social banking is not a new phenomenon in the finance landscape. The notion of social banking has its origins in religious and ethical movements and represents an alternative means of engaging in banking. Social banks grew exceptionally in the years of the financial crisis (Benedikter 2011; Weber 2011) and are considered an alternative and more resilient way of banking.

2.5   Social Banks: Definitions and Practices

The term "social banking"—also referred as "alternative", "ethical", "green", "sustainable", and "values-based" banking—describes banking and financial services designed to contribute to the development and prospering of people and the planet today and in the future (Institute for Social Banking 2017). As noted by Weber and Remer (2011) and by Tischer and Remer (2016), a clear definition of social banking does not exist, essentially because each alternative term used has a "slightly different center of gravity" by placing the focus on different aspects of social change and development (Benedikter 2011). Thus, De Clerck (2009, p. 214) states: "*Social, ethical, alternative, sustainable, development and solidarity banking and finance are denominations that are currently used to express particular ways of working with money, based on non-financial deliberations. A precise and unified definition of these types of finance as such is not available and perhaps not possible because of the different traditions from which ethical finance actors have emerged.*"

Weber and Remer (2011) highlight that "*social banking sounds like an oxymoron, combining what does not belong together. To others banking is inherently social and to them the phrase social banking is almost tautological.*

Some refer to social banks as those that serve socially oriented or charitable clients. Others use the term social banking to refer to banking based on the new social media, such as the Internet and related software. In some regions social banking is equated with government banking, in others it is equated with microfinance. Finally, some argue the social part in social banking could and should be replaced by sustainable or ethical, whilst others insist that these terms are not to be used interchangeably" (p. 1). Social banks are financial intermediaries that focus on noneconomic criteria (Cornée and Szafarz 2014) and that deliver financial services to individuals and organizations that have positive social, environmental, or sustainable impacts (Weber 2012; Weber and Duan 2012). Their business model is based on two principles: achieving a positive impact on society and achieving a sustainable financial return (Guene and Mayo 2001; Geobey and Weber 2013). Social banks follow the concepts of social finance and blended value and use business practices designed to generate social or environmental benefits (Weber 2011; Weber and Remer 2011; Weber and Duan 2012) by differing from traditional banks on a series of characteristics (e.g., legal status, size, and goals) (Benedikter 2011; Weber 2011). Milano (2011) identifies several types of social bank:

- Ethical and alternative banks
- Banks of philosophical/theological nature
- Banks of economic/social nature
- Microfinance institutions
- Banks that do not accept interest
- Children's banks

Benedikter (2011) identifies "financial humanism" as the constituent philosophy of social banking and highlights two major aspects to be considered to understand it: the importance of culture and the concept of ethics. The concept of culture is included in the concept of sustainability,[4] which implies a significant difference in respect of traditional banks that need to change their way of doing banking to be sustainable while social banks born around this concept. With regard to the second aspect, money is conceived not as a value itself but as the expression of a social relationship based on mutual trust and help. In particular,

Social banking is indeed decisively centered about changing the consciousness of consumers and the broad public regarding what money is and how it can be best used. Since it wants to provide and increase the societal insight into the connections between money, society, politics, culture, and education in order to reach out for a more just and balanced world, it follows the basic principles of enlightenment: rationalization and emancipation for the largest possible number of people. (Benedikter 2011, p. 50)

As described by Becchetti (2011), social banking entails a change in corporate goals so that they are based not on profit maximization but on the creation of social and environmental value together with economic value and distinguished for their driving principles: transparency, communication, and participation (Von Passavant 2011). These three principles are applied in all bank operations. The Institute for Social Banking highlights the following characteristics of social banks:

- Catalog of social, environmental, and ethical criteria to prevent or support activities that respectively harm or foster the common good
- Core banking—traditional banking practices and values; a focus on certain traditional activities—namely, in the savings and loans business
- Focus on the needs of communities in the real economy and civil society
- Nonmonetary values guiding all business activities
- Ownership structures preventing dependence on dominant individual interests
- Participatory organizational structures and customer relations
- Proactive dialog with stakeholders and engagement in public discourse
- Promotion of giving as a central ingredient of renewal and development
- Rejection of profit maximization principles and of speculative activities
- Strategies that limit risk exposure and ensure resilience
- Set salary ratios (top-bottom) of approximately 10:1 with no or a very limited and equitable bonus systems
- Transparency and accountability (Institute for Social Banking 2017).

However, the main feature of social banking is highlighted by Benedikter (2011), who explains how the triple bottom[5] line approach is integrated into social banking: *"social banks are defined by applying three different standards to judge investment and lending opportunities that take into account three different criterions, all of them equally considered:*

- *Profit (respectively, economic rationality; there can't be losses that threaten the development of the bank as a whole),*
- *Environment (natural habitat, protection, and sustainable handling of resources),*
- *People (the primacy of the community and the balanced advancement of society, seen as a whole)"* (Benedikter 2011, p. 51).

De Clerck (2009, p. 220) provides an overview of the most globally important social banks. In particular, the author lists the following:

- ShoreBank, USA
- GLS Bank, Germany
- Triodos Bank, UK
- Freie Gemeinschaftsbank in der Schweiz, Switzerland
- Merkur Bank, Denmark
- Wainwright Bank and Trust Cy, USA
- Alternative Bank Schweiz, Switzerland
- Cultura Sparebank, Norway
- Ekobanken, Sweden
- Banca Popolare Etica, Italy
- Charity Bank, UK

The phenomenon of social banking is not new to the finance landscape, but it grew exceptionally during the years of the financial crisis (Benedikter 2011; Weber 2011).[6] Indeed, in recent years, social banks have not been affected by the financial crisis in the same way that mainstream financial institutions have. Relaño (2011) highlights that although social banks and traditional universal banks are regulated by the same authorities, must abide by the same rules, and must compete within the same market, they are not the same type of financial institution. Traditional banks and social banks are completely different because the former focus on profit maximization while the latter aim to combine financial surpluses with social returns (Relaño 2011; Mykhayliv 2016).

Moreover, social banks, except to the extent required by regulators, are not typically active on the interbank or wholesale markets and finance themselves with customer deposits by seeking to invest in organizations with similar values, including making proportionate investments in other values-based banks (Benedikter 2011; The Vienna Group 2015).

2.6   Reconsidering Banking and Finance Research: Is It Time for a Kuhnian Revolution?

This chapter highlights how, following the 2007/2008 turmoil, academics are posing several questions on the role of finance in society by questioning the classical assumptions of neoclassical finance theory. The financial crisis is also a crisis of trust in the banking system (Sapienza and Zingales 2012) in terms of leading banking professionals, political control mechanisms, and the rationality of consumers and investors (Stückelberger 2012). An absence of diversity in research paradigms arguably translates into a body of knowledge that presents important limitations to attempting to make sense of important phenomena (Gendron and Smith-Lacroix 2015). The crisis cast doubt on finance studies that were often based on abstract mathematical and reductionist methods of research and limited by rigid models and theories (Colander et al. 2009).

Through the growing movement criticizing mainstream finance, several scholars argue that a significant diversification of the methods, concepts, and practical tools developed in academic finance is needed (Bay and Schinkus 2012; Alijani and Karyotis 2016; Lagoarde-Segot 2010, 2014, 2015; Paranque and Pérez 2016).[7] Critiques of traditional finance also refer to its epistemological approach. Lagoarde-Segot (2016) highlight that finance researchers "restrict their work to a monolithic approach derived from positivism" (p. 91) and that *"academic finance is indeed rooted in objectivist ontology: the financial world, just like the natural world, is assumed to be made of stable and tangible entities* (e.g., *financial markets, financial institutions, money…), which are external to the observer. Finance research considers that financial institutions (banks, money, markets…) and financial behavior (risk-return optimization) exist independently of individual or collective representations of the social world"* (p. 90). By using a positivist approach, modern finance does not include *"moral and ethical considerations and reflections on social well-being"* (Lagoarde-Segot 2015); in a neoclassical financial scheme, *"personal interactions and authority are absent. Consequently, all behavior is ethically neutral"* (Blommestein 2009, p. 72). In criticizing this methodological and epistemological approach, Lagoarde-Segot (2015) stresses that *"academic finance has moral, philosophical and political aspects"* (p. 97) and highlights that the subjectivist ontology represents a core assumption of the domain of finance that adopts methods of the social sciences. In this case, *"notions of ethics, values, and intentionality become key-concepts"* (Lagoarde-Segot 2015, p. 106). In particular, as stated by Gippel (2013), the 2007 financial crisis is viewed by many scholars as an "impetus to search for new paradigms and thus may be described in a Kuhnian sense as a *crisis"* (p. 128). From Kuhn's (1962) point of view, science progresses through *paradigm-shifting* and "normal" science. More specifically, Bloomfield (2010, p. 26) clarifies that *"a paradigm provides a theoretical framework for researchers to test and bolster (or modify) through what Kuhn* calls *"normal science"*. *Normal science establishes the validity of the paradigm but may also uncover anomalies —observations inconsistent with the paradigm. New paradigms become successful only if they can explain anomalies of sufficient quantity and importance in a sufficiently simple way"*. In this sense, a clear picture is provided by Stout (2005) who states that *"to describe the current state of finance in the terms of Thomas Kuhn's classic The Structure of Scientific Revolutions (1970), the old paradigm of an efficient market is crumbling. But the outlines of a new paradigm are visible in the resulting cloud of intellectual dust"*.

This intellectual dust is currently animated by academics who are trying to promote a paradigmatic shift that can surpass the limits and rigid assumptions of mainstream finance.

From the analysis of literature in the field of ethics and finance, one major question emerges: Are classical finance models able to depict what occurs in the real world? Several scholars have highlighted that the relationship between finance and ethics is still unresolved and find the source of this question in the methodological and epistemological basis of mainstream finance. Carè et al. (2018) describe how alternative finance is becoming more central by including eight emerging themes of finance research within this broader concept; they further highlight how the habitus of finance academics appears to be ready for a change despite historical resilience to new theories and knowledge. Among emerging trends, Carè et al. (2018) proposes social banking and social finance, which are considered to be relatively new developments in the international banking and finance landscape. The authors also stress that the increased number of papers published on this subject in recent years can be viewed as a sign of an understanding of the meaning, importance, and potential of this thematic area.

Despite the fact that the main objective of this chapter is not to provide an answer to this question, previous paragraphs tried to point out a series of insights on what is occurring in research on banking and finance. A Kuhnian revolution is a slow process, but the path has been opened. Indeed, the new and emerging fields of behavioral and social finance represent an attempt at a paradigmatic shift. Through this new lens, finance may be viewed as a means not only to maximize profits but also to benefit and positively impact society. In this sense, social finance represents not merely a new means of engaging in finance but an alternative way of thinking about finance.

Social finance scholars view social banking as a new alternative model to traditional banks. However, studies demonstrate that social banks are a typical European phenomenon with many years of history.

Social banking is not a new phenomenon, and we note that it comes from the ancient term "Monti di Pietà", but in this time period, characterized by the need for alternative business and finance models, social banks may represent an interesting source of learning. These banks are characterized by the aims declared in their own mission statements: to create a positive impact on society while running their operations in consideration of this aspect. This phenomenon should not be underestimated. Social banks have been resilient in times of crisis by doing something good, but they are a limited phenomenon, and their business approaches differ considerably from those of traditional banks.

APPENDIX 2.1: BANKING ON VALUE—THE CASE OF TRIODOS BANK AND CHARITY BANK

This section provides an overview of two social banks: Triodos Bank and Charity Bank. These cases are analyzed to highlight the main characteristics of social banks and of these two banks in particular.

The selection of cases is not random but rather follows an information-oriented selection approach (Flyvbjerg 2006). The cases are selected so that they are relatively similar in regard to the matter for analysis. This selection process highlighted Charity Bank in the United Kingdom and Triodos Bank based in the Netherlands as two very interesting cases. In particular, they provide extensive information about their impact measurement and reporting approaches.

The Case of Triodos Bank

Triodos Bank is a European social bank registered in the Netherlands, and since the 1980s, it has distinguished itself by specializing in financing innovative environmental and social enterprise initiatives with social and environmental aims (Cowton and Thompson 2001; De Clerck 2009; Dossa and Kaeufer 2014; Bouma et al. 2017). Triodos Bank had tried to position itself as a humanistic alternative to other banks to demonstrate that saving, investing, and lending can be combined with social and environmental progress (de Graaf 2012, p. 159). Many authors consider Triodos to be an excellent example of the European tradition of "social banking", which has evolved to meet the particular needs of the social economy that often face difficulties in obtaining finance from the traditional providers (Weber and Remer 2011; Cowton and Thompson 2001) by trying to restore a sense of relationship between depositors and borrowers which tends to be broken in conventional banking practice (Cowton 2002; Cowton and Thompson 2001). The Triodos website states:

> Triodos Bank was founded on sustainable principles, so sustainability is in our DNA. For us, sustainable banking means using money to bring about positive and lasting change; placing value on people and planet, as well as profit. We do that by financing companies, institutions and projects that add cultural value and benefit people and the environment, with the support of savers and investors who want to help make the world a better place – as well as a good return on their money. Crucially, our definition of sustainable banking means that this is all we do: we only invest in sustainable enterprises and we only use the money entrusted to us by savers and investors – just like banks used to do, in the days before derivatives and credit default swaps.

Triodos Bank's mission can be summarized as follows:

- To help create a society that promotes people's quality of life and that has human dignity at its core;
- to enable individuals, institutions, and businesses to use money more consciously in ways that benefit people and the environment and promote sustainable development; and
- to offer customers sustainable financial products and high-quality service (Triodos Bank Annual report 2016, 2017, p. 1).

Risk, Return, and Impact: The Triodos Approach
Triodos' business approach focuses on delivering sustainable social, environmental, and cultural impacts as well as risks and returns via the following business principles:

- Promoting sustainable development—considering the social, environmental, and financial impacts of everything we do;
- respecting and obeying the law—in every country where we do business;
- respecting human rights—of individuals, and within different societies and cultures; supporting the aims of the United Nation's Universal Declaration of Human Rights;

- respecting the environment—doing all we can to create and encourage positive environmental impacts;
- being accountable to all our stakeholders for all our actions; and
- continuous improvement—always looking for better ways of doing things in every area of our business (Triodos Bank Business Principles 2016b, p. 1)

Unlike traditional banks, which primarily focus on risks and returns to avoid negative outcomes and maximize returns to shareholders, Triodos Bank uses impact, risk, and return from a long-term perspective (Triodos Bank Annual Report 2015, 2016a). Triodos' investment strategy revolves around six main sectors:

- Energy and climate
- Emerging markets
- Inclusive finance
- Sustainable food and agriculture
- Arts and culture
- Sustainable real estate
- Socially responsible investments

Triodos Investment Management[8] also invests in listed companies with above-average environmental, social, and governance (ESG) performance.

Risk Management

The aim of Triodos Bank's risk management activities is to ensure the long-term resilience of the business (Triodos Bank Annual Report 2016, 2017). Its risk appetite is based on three objectives that complement its goals and guarantee a sustainable banking model. They are to (1) protect the bank's identity and reputation, (2) maintain healthy balance sheet relations, and (3) maintain stable growth. A risk governance framework and a three-line defense model have been put in place. The three lines of defense model involves

- first-line functions: responsible for managing the risks of operations;
- second-line functions: ensure that risks are appropriately identified and managed; and
- the third line of defense: (the internal audit function) provides independent and objective assurance of Triodos Bank's corporate governance, internal controls, compliance and risk management systems.

The director of risk and compliance is fully responsible for second-line risk management and compliance activities and reports directly to the chief financial officer. Such activities are supervised by the Audit and Risk Committee of the Supervisory Board.

Impact

Under the Global Alliance for Banking on Value (GABV),[9] Triodos Bank has developed an impact scorecard that is designed to measure

- basic requirements of a sustainable bank such as its mission and approach to transparency;
- quantitative factors, such as the proportion of the bank's assets committed to the real economy; and
- qualitative elements that provide an account of how a bank translates its sustainability agenda into its actual work.

Return

In recent years, Triodos Bank has faced stiff competition from conventional banks showing a growing interest in sustainability as a market opportunity. Despite this, Triodos continued to grow its sustainable loan portfolio by 13% in 2015. Its total loan portfolio, which includes short-term lending to municipalities, increased by 22% while its assets under management grew by 19% in 2015 (Triodos Bank Annual Report 2016, 2017).

The Case of Charity Bank

Charity Bank was founded in 2002 to support charities and social enterprises with loans and to provide people with opportunities to save in line with their values (Charity Bank 2017/2018 Loans Portfolio Report 2017a). Charity Bank was founded with the charitable mission to lend money to charities and social enterprises, and it was the first charity to be granted a banking license from the Financial Services Authority, rendering it unique as the only not-for-profit bank lending exclusively to charities (Buttle 2008). Shareholders are led by Big Society Capital and the Charities Aid Foundation and include a number of charitable trusts and foundations (Charity Bank Annual Report 2016, 2017b) that are committed to supporting the social sector. Charity Bank's balance sheet increased by 15.3% during 2016, while on the assets side, loans to charities, community groups, and social enterprises increased by 27.9%, with 72.8% of the balance sheet being used to make charitable loans. With respect to liabilities, deposit levels increased over the years, growing by 12.9% in 2016 (Charity Bank Annual Report 2016, 2017b). Charity Bank's principal risks and uncertainties lie in its exposure to

- the political and economic environment and changes in the government's approach to social policy;
- credit risk and the concentration of such exposure in one sector, with a resulting lack of portfolio diversification;
- a mismatch between the tenor of its loans and the maturity of its deposits and the risk of depositors withdrawing deposits upon notice ("liquidity risk");
- interest rate mismatches on its assets and liabilities;
- funding risk and particularly the need to fund increases in the loan book via capital raising and deposits from savers; and
- key person dependencies arising from its small size (Charity Bank Annual Report 2016, 2017b).

Social Impact Assessment

Charity Bank seeks both social and financial returns and has systems and processes to ensure that its decision-making processes help it achieve both (Charity Bank Social Impact Statement 2017e). The bank assesses the social impacts of the organizations to which it lends by considering how the organization will benefit of the loan and how the people it is working with will benefit of the loan (Charity Bank Measuring our social impact 2017d). In doing this, the bank considers three areas that are most relevant to its borrowers:

- *Mission focus*—Does the organization have a clear idea of what it is trying to achieve?
- *Organizational capacity*—Does the organization have people with the right expertise and sound systems of governance?
- *Financial resources*—Does the organization have the finances necessary to service the loan and meet its business plan objectives? (Charity Bank Social Impact Statement 2017e).

Table 2.1 presents an overview of sectors through which Charity Bank grants loans.

Table 2.1   Charity Bank: Loans per sector since 2002

Sector	Amount of money	Number of loans
Arts	10.998.080£	75
Community	28.153.154	173
Education and training	17.219.737	89
Environment	9.265.037	54
Faith	24.929.167	93
Health and social care	33.691.502	154
Social housing	62.398.181	184
Sport	8.402.945	54
Total	195.057.803	876

As of September 2017

Source: Charity Bank website (https://charitybank.org)

Loans are granted to the following types of organizations:

- Loans for any purpose and on any terms to any entity that is itself a charity and provides a public benefit;
- loans for any purpose and on any terms to any entity that meets Charity Bank's criteria as a social sector organization;
- loans on a mixed-motive basis where there is more than an incidental noncharitable (or private) benefit; and
- loans to other organizations without a charitable purpose and that are not social sector organizations under circumstances where the potential borrower can adequately demonstrate to Charity Bank that
  - the loan, if drawn, will facilitate material worthwhile social impact that could not otherwise be achieved or is a refinancing of such a loan;
  - the borrower passes Charity Bank's due diligence process; and
  - the loan documentation incorporates protections to maintain the organization's commitment to its intended social impacts or requires Charity Bank to be prepaid if it ceases to maintain its stance on supporting social impacts (Charity Bank CSR Policy 2017c).

Looking for Similarities and Differences

Although both Charity Bank and Triodos Bank can be classified as social banks, they have different characteristics and mission statements. Triodos Bank delivers retail banking services (e.g., payment cards) in addition to loans and investment funds, while Charity Bank delivers savings accounts and loans to charities while actively excluding loans made to for-profit

Table 2.2 Mission statements and impact assessments of Charity Bank and Triodos Bank

	Charity Bank	*Triodos Bank*
Mission	To lend money to charities and social enterprises	To help create a society that promotes people's quality of life and that values human dignity at its core To enable individuals, institutions and businesses to use money more consciously in ways that benefit people and the environment while promoting sustainable development To offer customers sustainable financial products and high-quality services
Impact assessment	The bank assesses the social impacts of organizations to which it lends by considering how organizations will benefit from loans given.	Impact scorecard

Source: Our elaboration

enterprises. This is a crucial difference and implies that Charity Bank will refuse certain projects that may be accepted by Triodos Bank. Table 2.2 highlights the main differences in terms of mission statements and impact assessments.

Despite their many differences, Triodos Bank and Charity Bank have a common claim of contributing to positive social and environmental outcomes. Transparency is a strong value attached to their business activities. Both banks provide information on specific projects that they lend to through storytelling.

Notes

1. The principal features of financialization include (1) the increased significance of the financial sector relative to the real sector; (2) the transfer of income from the real sector to the financial sector; and (3) increased income inequality and wage stagnation (Palley 2013).
2. On the concept of EMH as an artificial construct, see Howden (2009).
3. Several authors note that the academic literature on the topic of social finance is limited and "under-theorized and in need of conceptual framing" (Nicholls 2010; Antadze and Westley 2012). New academicinstitutions such as the Skoll Centre for Social Entrepreneurship at the Said Business School

of Oxford University in 2003, the Waterloo Institute for Social Innovation and Resilience (WISIR), and the Liege UniversityCentre for Social Economy have been established. This trend is not only attributable to increased interest from academics in innovations in the financial sphere but also to a growing awareness that investment insound academic research and teaching is a decisive pillar for developing mainstream "cultural" attitudes toward money and finance in a more inclusive and balanced direction.

4. On the concept of banking humanism, see Pirson et al. (2016).

5. For further information on the triple bottom line, see, among others, Elkington (2002) and Willard (2012).

6. On the origins of social banks, further information may be retrieved from Maccarini and Prandini 2009; Becchetti 2011; Benedikter 2011; Milano 2011; Weber 2011; Weber and Remer 2011; Weber and Duan 2012; and Weber 2016.

7. On the need to reconsider the role of finance studies and following a seminar held at the KEDGE Business School in Marseille (France) in May 2015, the "Postcrisis Finance Research Manifesto" was launched, and it states: "The ongoing economic, social and environmental crisis has revealed the need to redefine the function of finance. Academic finance bears significant responsibility in this process addressing the interaction between finance and society. As a response, many private actors have broadened their definition of 'value' in order to include environmental and social elements into their management and asset allocation practices. Such practices, however, appear incompatible with the current theoretical and methodological foundations of academic mainstream finance, which is heavily influenced by logical positivism and the methodological individualism hypothesis based on the maximization of the shareholder utility function. Academic finance focuses on the micro level and emphasizes econometric modelling rather than adopting a longer-run view incorporating the lessons from economic history. This paradox challenges us to reconsider the epistemological and theoretical foundations of modern finance, and, in particular, the dominant role played by shareholders. It is our responsibility to question the idea that social welfare and ethics are simply the result of shareholders value maximization and to enrich finance research, particularly with perspectives and contributions from other social sciences" (Lagoarde-Segot 2017, p. 122).

3. Triodos Investment Management is a globally active impact investor that includes Triodos Investment Management BV and Triodos Investment & Advisory Services BV, which are both fully owned subsidiaries of Triodos Bank NV.

9. The Global Alliance for Banking on Values is an independent network of banks founded in 2009 that use finance to deliver sustainable economic, social, and environmental development outcomes. For further information, see: http://www.gabv.org.

REFERENCES

Alijani, S., & Karyotis, C. (2016). *Sustainability: Finance, economy, and society.* Bingley: Emerald Group Publishing.

Altman, M. (2004). The Nobel Prize in behavioral and experimental economics: A contextual and critical appraisal of the contributions of Daniel Kahneman and Cernon Smith. *Review of Political Economy, 16*(1), 3–41.

Altman, M. (2005). The ethical economy and competitive markets: Reconciling altruistic, moralistic, and ethical behavior with the rational economic agent and competitive markets. *Journal of Economic Psychology, 26*(5), 732–757.

Antadze, N., & Westley, F. R. (2012). Impact metrics for social innovation: Barriers or bridges to radical change? *Journal of Social Entrepreneurship, 3*(2), 133–150.

Bay, T., & Schinkus, C. (2012). Critical finance studies: A manifesto for an interdisciplinary perspective. *Journal of Interdisciplinary Economics, 24*, 1–6.

Becchetti, L. (2011). Why do we need social banking? In S. Remer & O. Weber (Eds.), *Social banks and the future of sustainable finance.* London/New York: Taylor & Francis.

Benedikter, R. (2011). Social banking and social finance. In R. Benedikter (Ed.), *Social banking and social finance* (SpringerBriefs in Business). New York: Springer.

Bettner, M., McGoun, E., & Robinson, C. (1994). The case for qualitative research in finance. *International Review of Financial Analysis, 3*(1), 1–18.

Blommestein, H. J. (2009). *The financial crisis as a symbol of the failure of academic finance?(A methodological digression).* Retrieved from https://papers.ssrn.com/sol3/papers.cfm?abstract_id=1477399

Bloomfield, R. J. (2010). *Traditional vs. behavioral finance* (Johnson School Research Paper Series, (22-2010)). New York: Cornell University.

Boatright, J. R. (2010). *Finance ethics: Critical issues in theory and practice* (Vol. 11). Hoboken: Wiley.

Bouma, J. J., Jeucken, M., & Klinkers, L. (Eds.). (2017). *Sustainable banking: The greening of finance.* New York: Routledge.

Buttle, M. (2008). Diverse economies and the negotiations and practices of ethical finance: The case of Charity Bank. *Environment and Planning A, 40*(9), 2097–2113.

Carè, R., Trotta, A., & Rizzello, A. (2018). An alternative finance approach for a more sustainable financial system. In *Designing a sustainable financial system: Development goals and socio-ecological responsibility.* Basingstoke: Palgrave Macmillan.

Charity Bank. (2017a). *A bank for good – 2017/18 Loan Portfolio Report.* Tonbridge.

Charity Bank. (2017b). *Annual report 2016.* Tonbridge.

Charity Bank. (2017c). *Corporate social responsibility policy.* Tonbridge.

Charity Bank. (2017d). *Measuring social impact: Our approach.* Tonbridge.

Charity Bank. (2017e). *Social impact statement.* Tonbridge.

Colander, D., Goldberg, M., Haas, A., Juselius, K., Kirman, A., Lux, T., & Sloth, B. (2009). The financial crisis and the systemic failure of the economics profession. *Critical Review, 21*(2–3), 249–267.

Cornée, S., & Szafarz, A. (2014). Vive la différence: Social banks and reciprocity in the credit market. *Journal of Business Ethics, 125*(3), 361–380.

Cowton, C. J. (2002). Integrity, responsibility and affinity: Three aspects of ethics in banking. *Business Ethics: A European Review, 11*(4), 393–400.

Cowton, C. J., & Thompson, P. (2001). Financing the social economy: A case study of Triodos Bank. *International Journal of Nonprofit and Voluntary Sector Marketing, 6*(2), 145–155.

da Silva, A. F. (2007). Social banking: The need of the hour. In *Social banking-Perspectives and experiences* (pp. 3–9). Hyderabad: Icfai University Press.

De Clerck, F. (2009). Ethical banking. In *Ethical prospects* (pp. 209–227). Netherlands: Springer.

de Graaf, F. J. (2012). Triodos Bank—Mission-driven success pays off: From Dutch enfant terrible to European business leader. In H. Spitzeck, M. Pirson, & C. Dierksmeier (Eds.), *Banking with Integrity* (Humanism in Business Series). London: Palgrave Macmillan.

Dembinski, P. H. (2009). *Finance: Servant or Deceiver?* Observatoire de la Finance.

Dobson, J. (1991). Reconciling financial economics and business ethics. *Business & Professional Ethics Journal, 10*, 23–42.

Dobson, J. (1997). *Finance ethics: The rationality of virtue.* Lanham: Rowman & Littlefield.

Dobson, J. (2010). Behavioral assumptions of finance. *Finance Ethics: Critical Issues in Theory and Practice*, 45–61.

Dossa, Z., & Kaeufer, K. (2014). Understanding sustainability innovations through positive ethical networks. *Journal of Business Ethics, 119*(4), 543–559.

Edery, Y. (2006). Ethical developments in finance: Implications for charities and social enterprise. *Social Enterprise Journal, 2*(1), 82–100.

Elkington, J. (2002). The triple bottom line. In M. V. Russo (Ed.), *Environmental management: Readings and cases.* Thousand Oaks: Sage.

Etzioni, A. (1988). *The moral dimension: Toward a new economics.* New York: Free Press.

Fabozzi, F. J., Focardi, S. M., & Jonas, C. (2014). *Investment management: A science to teach or an art to learn?* Charlottesville: Research Foundation of CFA Institute.

Findlay, M. C., & Williams, E. E. (1985). A Post Keynesian view of modern financial economics: In search of alternative paradigms. *Journal of Business Finance and Accounting, 12*(1), Spring, 1–18.

Flyvbjerg, B. (2006). Five misunderstandings about case-study research. *Qualitative Inquiry, 12*(2), 219–245.

Freeman, R. E. (1994). The politics of stakeholder theory: Some future directions. *Business Ethics Quarterly, 4*, 409–421.

Gendron, Y., & Smith-Lacroix, J. H. (2015). The global financial crisis: Essay on the possibility of substantive change in the discipline of finance. *Critical Perspectives on Accounting, 30*, 83–101.

Geobey, S., & Weber, O. (2013). Lessons in operationalizing social finance: The case of Vancouver City Savings Credit Union. *Journal of Sustainable Finance & Investment, 3*(2), 124–137.

Gippel, J. K. (2013). A revolution in finance? *Australian Journal of Management, 38*(1), 125–146.

Guene, C., & Mayo, E. (2001). Introduction: A problem here to stay. In *Banking and social cohesion: Alternative responses to a global market* (pp. 1–10). Charlbury: Jon Carpenter Publishing.

Hangl, C. (2014). A literature review about the landscape of social finance. *Journal of Finance and Risk Perspectives, 3*(4), 64–98.

Harji, K., & Hebb, T. (2010). *Investing for impact: Issues and opportunities for social finance in Canada.* Ottawa: Carleton Centre for Community Innovation.

Henrich, J. (2004). Cultural group selection, coevolutionary processes and large-scale cooperation. *Journal of Economic Behavior & Organization, 53*(1), 3–35.

Höchstädter, A. K., & Scheck, B. (2015). What's in a name: An analysis of impact investing understandings by academics and practitioners. *Journal of Business Ethics, 132*(2), 449–475.

Howden, D. (2009). Fama's efficient market hypothesis and Mises's evenly rotating economy: Comparative constructs. *Quarterly Journal of Austrian Economics, 12*(2), 3.

Hsieh, N. (2010). Efficiency and rationality. In J. Boatright (Ed.), *Finance ethics: Critical issues in theory and practice* (p. 2010). Hoboken: Wiley.

Institute for Social Banking. (2017). *Value based banking. Bringing the voice of the citizen into finance.* Retrieved from https://www.google.it/url?sa=t&rct=j&q=&esrc=s&source=web&cd=1&cad=rja&uact=8&ved=0ahUKEwivsNOKzPDXAhXQ1qQKHW4gAk4QFggqMAA&url=https%3A%2F%2Fwww.social-banking.org%2Fwp-content%2Fuploads%2F2017%2F08%2FValues_Based_Banking_pdf-1.pdf&usg=AOvVaw2AXuj8hXrPlcmwOZEHDF8n

Jorion, P. (2009). Risk management lessons from the credit crisis. *European Financial Management, 15*(5), 923–933.

Joy, I., de Las Casas, L., Rickey, B., & Capital, N. P. (2011). *Understanding the demand for and supply of social finance*. London: New Philanthropy Capital.

Kahneman, D., Knetch, J. L., & Thaler, R. H. (1986a). Fairness as a constraint on profit seeking: Entitlements in the market. *American Economic Review, 76,* 728–741.

Kahneman, D., Knetch, J. L., & Thaler, R. H. (1986b). Fairness and the assumptions of economics. *Journal of Business, 59*(4, Part 2), S285–S300.

Keasey, K., & Hudson, R. (2007). Finance theory: A house without windows. *Critical Perspectives on Accounting, 18*(8), 932–951.

Kirman, A. (2010). The economic crisis is a crisis for economic theory. *CESifo Economic Studies, 56*(4), 498–535.

Kolb, R. W. (2010). Ethical implications of finance. *Finance Ethics: Critical Issues in Theory and Practice,* 21–43.

Krugman, P. (2014, September 14). How to get it wrong. *The New York Times.*

Kuhn, T. S. (1962). *The structure of scientific revolutions.* Chicago: University of Chicago Press.

Lagoarde-Segot, T. (2010). *After the crisis: Rethinking finance.* New York: Nova Science.

Lagoarde-Segot, T. (2014). *La finance solidaire, un humanisme économique.* Brussels: De Boeck.

Lagoarde-Segot, T. (2015). Diversifying finance research: From financialization to sustainability. *International Review of Financial Analysis, 39,* 1–6.

Lagoarde-Segot, T. (2016). Prolegomena to an alternative study of finance. *In Finance reconsidered: New perspectives for a responsible and sustainable finance* (pp. 89–110). Bingley: Emerald Group Publishing Limited.

Lagoarde-Segot, T. (2017). Financialization: Towards a new research agenda. *International Review of Financial Analysis, 51,* 113–123.

Lagoarde-Segot, T., & Paranque, B. (2017). Sustainability and the reconstruction of academic finance. *Research in International Business and Finance, 39,* 657–662.

Lawson, T. (2009). The current economic crisis: Its nature and the course of academic economics. *Cambridge Journal of Economics, 33*(4), 759–777.

Lehner, O. M., & Nicholls, A. (2014). Social finance and crowdfunding for social enterprises: A public–private case study providing legitimacy and leverage. *Venture Capital, 16*(3), 271–286.

Lewis, V., Kay, K. D., Kelso, C., & Larson, J. (2010). Was the 2008 financial crisis caused by a lack of corporate ethics? *Global Journal of Business Research, 2*(4), 77–84.

Maccarini, A. M., & Prandini, R. (2009). Building civil society through finance: The Ethical Bank in Italy. *Italian Journal of Sociology of Education, 1*(2), 54–107.

McCosh, A. M. (1999). *Financial ethics.* Boston: Kluwer Academic Publishers.

Milano, R. (2011). Social banking: A brief history. *Social Banks and the Future of Sustainable Finance, 64*, 15–47.

Moore, M. L., Westley, F. R., & Brodhead, T. (2012). Social finance intermediaries and social innovation. *Journal of Social Entrepreneurship, 3*(2), 184–205.

Mykhayliv, D. (2016). *The economic efficiency and profitability of social banks.* Foundation for European Progressive Studies. Retrieved from http://www.feps-europe.eu/en/publications/details/430

Nicholls, A. (2010). The institutionalization of social investment: The interplay of investment logics and investor rationalities. *Journal of Social Entrepreneurship, 1*(1), 70–100.

Nicholls, A., & Pharoah, C. (2007). *The landscape of social investment: A holistic topology of opportunities and challenges.* Oxford: Skoll Centre for Social Entrepreneurship.

Oberlechner, T. (2007). *The psychology of ethics in the finance and investment industry.* Charlottesville: Research Foundation of CFA Institute.

Palley, T. I. (2013). Financialization: What it is and why it matters. In T. I. Palley (Ed.), *Financialization* (pp. 17–40). Basingstoke: Palgrave Macmillan.

Paranque, B., & Pérez, R. (2016). Finance reconsidered: New perspectives for a responsible and sustainable finance. In *Finance reconsidered: New perspectives for a responsible and sustainable finance* (pp. 3–13). Bingley: Emerald Group Publishing Limited.

Pirson, M., Gangahar, A., & Wilson, F. (2016). Humanistic and economistic approaches to banking–better banking lessons from the financial crisis? *Business Ethics: A European Review, 25*(4), 400–415.

Porter, M. E., & Kramer, M. R. (2011). Creating shared value. *Harvard Business Review, 89*(1–2), 62–77.

Preda, A. (2017). The sciences of finance, their boundaries, their values. In E. Ippoliti & P. Chen (Eds.), *Methods and finance* (Studies in Applied Philosophy, Epistemology and Rational Ethics, Vol. 34). Cham: Springer.

Prentice, R. A. (2007). Ethical decision making: More needed than good intentions. *Financial Analysts Journal, 63*(6), 17–30.

Rappaport, A., & Bogle, J. C. (2011). *Saving capitalism from short-termism: How to build long-term value and take back our financial future.* New York: McGraw Hill Professional.

Relaño, F. (2011). Maximizing social return in the banking sector. *Corporate Governance: The International Journal of Business in Society, 11*(3), 274–284.

Sandberg, J. (2008). Understanding the separation thesis. *Business Ethics Quarterly, 18*(2), 213–232.

San-Jose, L., & Retolaza, J. L. (2017). Ethics in finance research: Recommendations from an academic experts Delphi panel. *Journal of Academic Ethics, 1*, 1–20.

Sapierza, P., & Zingales, L. (2012). A trust crisis. *International Review of Finance, 12*(2), 123–131.

Shefrin, H., & Statman, M. (2000). Behavioral portfolio theory. *Journal of Financial and Quantitative Analysis, 35*(2), 127–151.

Shiller, R. J. (2013). *Finance and the good society.* Princeton: Princeton University Press.

Smith, C. W., Jr. (1990). Introduction. In *The modern theory of corporate finance* (2nd ed., pp. 3–24). New York: McGraw-Hill Publishing Company.

Stout, L. A. Forthcoming. Inefficient markets and the new finance. *Journal of Financial Transformation.* Available at SSRN: https://ssrn.com/abstract=729224

Stückelberger, C. (2012). Credo+ Credibility= Credit. *Trust and Ethics in Finance, 2012,* 43–45.

Szyszka, A. (2011). The genesis of the 2008 global financial crisis and challenges to the neoclassical paradigm of finance. *Global Finance Journal, 22*(3), 211–216.

The Vienna Group. (2015). *Values based banking. Bringing the voice of the citizen into finance* (Working Paper 15/03 prepared for the UNEP Inquiry). Retrieved from http://unepinquiry.org/wp-content/uploads/2015/04/Values_Based_Banking.pdf

Tischer, D., & Remer, S. (2016). Growing social banking through (business) associations. In O. M. Lehner (Ed.), *Routledge handbook of social and sustainable finance.* Londom/New York: Routledge.

Triodos Bank. (2016a). *Annual report 2015.*

Triodos Bank. (2016b). *Business principles 2016.*

Triodos Bank. (2017). *Annual report 2016.*

Van Hoorn, A. (2015). The global financial crisis and the values of professionals in finance: An empirical analysis. *Journal of Business Ethics, 130*(2), 253–269.

Vandemeulebroucke, V., Beck, K., & Kauefer, K. (2010). *Networking social finance.* Brussels: INAISE.

Vasle, D., Sebastian, T. C., & Radu, T. (2011). A behavioral approach to the global financial crisis. *Economic Science, 20*(2), 340–346.

von Passavant, C. (2011). Inside social banks. In O. Weber & S. Remer (Eds.), *Social banks and the future of sustainable finance.* New York: Routledge.

Weber, O. (2011). *Mission and profitability of social banks* (Working Paper). Retrieved from https://papers.ssrn.com/sol3/papers2.cfm?abstract_id=1957637

Weber, O. (2012). *Social finance and impact investing* (Working Paper). Retrieved from https://ssrn.com/abstract=2160403

Weber, O. (2016). *The sustainability performance of Chinese Banks: Institutional impact.* Retrieved from https://papers.ssrn.com/sol3/papers.cfm?abstract_id=2752439

Weber, O., & Duan, Y. (2012). Social finance and banking. In H. K. Baker & J. R. Nofsinger (Eds.), *Socially responsible finance and investing: Financial institutions, corporations, investors, and activists* (pp. 161–180). Hoboken: Wiley.

Weber, O., & Remer, S. (Eds.). (2011). *Social banks and the future of sustainable finance*. New York: Routledge.

Werhane, P. H., & Freeman, R. E. (1999). Business ethics: The state of the art. *International Journal of Management Reviews, 1*(1), 1–16.

Wicks, A. C. (1996). Overcoming the separation thesis: The need for a reconsideration of business and society research. *Business & Society, 35*(1), 39–118.

Willard, B. (2012). *The new sustainability advantage: Seven business case benefits of a triple bottom line*. New York: New Society Publishers.

Zingales, L. (2015). *Does finance benefit society?* (No. w20894). Cambridge: National Bureau of Economic Research.

CHAPTER 3

Exploring the Role of Banks in Sustainable Development

Abstract This chapter highlights the contribution of financial systems to sustainable development and provides an excursus of the major changes that have occurred at the international level and that are a result of the increased attention banks have given to sustainability issues. The chapter also introduces the role of corporate social responsibility (CSR) practices in sustainability, focusing on the role of the credit risk management process and describing how sustainability issues might create value for banks.

Keywords Sustainable development • Sustainable banking • Environmental credit risk management • CSR • Disclosure • Risk management

3.1 Introduction

Banking failure and financial scandals that have occurred around the world brought about the need to rethink the role of banks in the society (Shiller 2013). In recent years, banks have been pressured by stakeholders to engage in social and environmental responsibility. Academia has focused on the relationship between sustainable development and finance (Jeucken 2010; Weber and Remer 2011), and environmental and social responsibility (Scholtens 2009) or irresponsibility (Herzig and Moon 2013), in the case of both banks and financial institutions. It is worth noting that many works emphasize that sustainability can be useful to improve the stability of the financial system (Liu 2012; Alexander 2014), and that sustainability

© The Author(s) 2018
R. Carè, *Sustainable Banking*,
https://doi.org/10.1007/978-3-319-73389-0_3

and ethical values can play a key role in finance (Lehner 2016). Sustainability is an important issue for national governments, and socially responsible companies may support governmental efforts in addressing goals like social and environmental development (Pichler and Lehner 2017). In this new scenario, banks must demonstrate that they take ethics and responsibility seriously by restoring their role as financial intermediaries that serve the economy (Weber and Feltmate 2016), thus moving toward a more sustainable business model.

The aim of this chapter is to provide an overview of the role that banks can play in sustainable development and of the major challenges and opportunities that emerge from this new business approach. For this purpose, the chapter highlights the contribution of the financial systems toward sustainable development and provides an excursus of the major changes that have occurred at the international level and that are the result of the increased attention banks have given to sustainability issues. Then, the chapter introduces the role of corporate social responsibility (CSR) practices in sustainability by focusing on the role of the credit risk management process. Finally, the last part describes how sustainability issues might create value for banks.

3.2   Toward a New Sustainable Approach

Sustainable finance has been defined as "*the provision of financial capital and risk management products and services in ways that promote or do not harm economic prosperity, the ecology and community well-being*" (Strandberg 2005, p. 6; IFC 2007). The website of the Swiss Finance Institute (SFI 2016) posted a note emphasizing its main characteristics: "*The two most common aspects of sustainable finance are that they have to do with: 1) lasting and long-term impact, or the sustainability factor, 2) and the interrelationship between environmental, social, and governance (ESG) issues, on the one hand, and financial issues such as financing, lending, and investment decisions, on the other.*" Therefore, in this vein, according to SFI (2016), "*sustainable finance is not only concerned with how financing and investment decisions influence ESG issues, but also with how ESG issues might influence investment decisions and asset valuations.*"

Currently, there is agreement that the concept of sustainable development is presented as the intersection between environment, society, and economy, which have been conceived in the past century as separate although connected entities (Giddings et al. 2002).

The concept of sustainability emerged in the 1970s in response to the understanding that "modern development practices were leading to worldwide environmental and social crises" (Wheeler 2013, p. 19).

The contribution of financial systems to sustainable development is significant considering the role that they play in society (Weber and Feltmate 2016; Bouma et al. 2017). Every financial system operating in a market-based economy performs five basic functions: running the payment system, providing liquidity, collecting and allocating new savings (from surplus units to deficit units), monitoring and disciplining users of externally raised savings, and pricing and redistributing risk (Rybczynski 1997). A detailed and comprehensive review of banking theory and a broad analysis of the question why internal financial institutions exist in the financial market is provided by Santomero (1984). In particular, the author highlights three different approaches: the first refers to the role of banks as asset transformers, the second points out the nature of the liabilities issued by banks and their central place in a monetary economy, and the third emphasizes the two-sided (assets and liabilities) nature of banks as critical explanations or rationales for their existence (Santomero 1984).

By acting as financial intermediary, banks have four major functions: (1) to transform money by scale, (2) to transform money by duration, (3) to transform money by spatial location/place, and (4) to act as assessors of risk (Jeucken 2010; Saunders and Cornett 2013; Cooperman 2016; Bouma et al. 2017). The intermediation role places banks in the position of influencing economic growth both in a quantitative and in a qualitative manner, and their financing policies are a way to create opportunities for sustainable business (Jeucken 2010; Bouma et al. 2017; Schaltegger et al. 2017).

3.3   THE INCREASED ATTENTION OF BANKS TOWARD SUSTAINABILITY ISSUES: FROM VOLUNTARY INITIATIVES TO MANDATORY REGULATION

The banking sectors' participation in sustainable and environmental issues began only recently. According to the most prominent literature of the 1990s and 2000s, banks began to address sustainability by considering first environmental and then social issues (Jeucken 2010; Viganò and Nicolai 2009). The financial sector was explicitly brought on board for the first time in the late 1990s (Jeucken 2010), when environment legislation had increased and many banks had developed more sophisticated risk assessment procedures, CSR practices, and risks agendas (Coulson and O'Sullivan 2014). More specifically, bankers started to familiarize themselves with environmental issues related to operations in 1991 when a small group of commercial banks, including Deutsche Bank, HSBC Holdings, Natwest, Royal Bank of Canada, and Westpac, participated in the United Nations Environment Programme Finance Initiative (UNEP FI) (Yüksel 2016; Schaltegger et al. 2017). The UNEP FI promoted the integration of environmental considerations into the financial sector's operations and services (Yüksel 2016), beginning with the concept that economic development needs to be compatible with human welfare and a healthy environment. To date, the UNEP FI has over 200-member institutions from over 40 countries.

In 2015, the UNEP FI's banking and investment members launched the Positive Impact Manifesto as a call for a new financing paradigm and with the aim of bridging the funding gap for sustainable development. Positive Impact Finance is defined in the Manifesto as *"that which verifiably produces a positive impact on the economy, society or the environment once any potential negative impacts have been duly identified and mitigated"* (UNEP FI 2015, p. 2). The development of a dedicated set of Principles for Positive Impact Finance that guide financiers and investors in their efforts to increase their positive impact on the economy, society, and the environment constitutes a central component of the Positive Impact Roadmap outlined in the Manifesto. The Principles for Positive Impact Finance was released in 2017 by the Positive Impact Working Group, which includes Australian Ethical, Banco Itaú, BNP Paribas, BMCE Bank of Africa, Caisse des Dépôts Group, Desjardins Group, First Rand, Hermes Investment Management, ING, Mirova, NedBank, Pax World, Piraeus Bank, SEB, Société Générale, Standard Bank, Triodos Bank, Westpac, and YES Bank. The principles are not sector based and are applicable to all forms of financial institutions and financial instruments (UNEP FI 2017).[1]

In addition, voluntary initiatives such as the OECD Principles, the UN Global Compact or the IFC (World Bank Group) encourage firms to integrate social aspects in their governance agenda and recognize that a company's environmental, social, and governance responsibilities are integral to its performance and long-term sustainability (White 2006; Walls et al. 2012).

A variety of guidelines or frameworks for reporting on sustainability such as the Global Reporting Initiative (GRI) and the International Organization for Standardization (ISO) 26000 are currently available (Weber and Feltmate 2016). The GRI and ISO frameworks are detailed in Chap. 4.

3.3.1   The Changing Legal Framework

Banks—and in general companies—are subject to a wide range of federal, state, and local environmental laws and regulations that can be classified as follows:

- Mandatory: regulations are mandatory requirements that enable banks and FIs to consider environmental/sustainability issues in a structured way in their overall credit appraisal processes and/or investment activities/practices.
- Voluntary: regulations provide banks with guidance on issues they need to be mindful of by taking the environmental and social dimensions of development into account in the conduct of their business activities. The intention is that, with the assistance of these banking sector basic sustainability principles, banks will be able to more systematically manage environmental and social predictability, transparency, and monitoring of their activities.

The following sections try to highlight the main legal frameworks under which Banks around the globe currently operate.

3.3.2   The United States

Based on the "polluter pays" principle, the Comprehensive Environmental Response, Compensation, and Liability Act (CERCLA) of 1980 was instituted in the United States in 1980 and primarily aimed at securing financing for soil remediation moving from the considerations that banks could be held liable in certain situations for the activities that they financed (Jeucken 2010; Case 1999; Weber and Remer 2011). CERCLA is considered as the moment in which banks began to pay close attention to the potential legal risks related to the environmental performance of the recipients of bank loans or credit (Zhang et al. 2011).

3.3.3   Canada

The Canadian banking sector is considered one of the most healthy, resilient, and safe globally (Chapman and Damar 2015), with financing activities that span all sectors of the economy, making banks particularly vulnerable to climate change-related risks (CSA 2010). Canadian Banks with equity greater than $1 billion are obliged to publish a public accountability statement that is regularly reviewed by the Department of Finance of the Government of Canada (Weber 2012). In particular, since 2010, the Canadian Securities Administrators (CSA) provided new guidance on disclosure requirements relating to environmental matters under securities legislation. This applies to all Canadian and foreign "reporting issuers", including all companies listed on Canadian stock exchanges. The CSA detailed the disclosure rules in the following areas:

1. Environmental risks and related matters
2. Environmental risk oversight and management
3. Forward-looking information requirements as they relate to environmental goals and targets
4. Impact of adoption of International Financial Reporting Standards (IFRS) on disclosure of environmental liabilities (CSA 2010).

In 2017, the CSA announced a project to review the disclosure of risks and financial impacts associated with climate change.

3.3.4   Brazil

In the context of country-specific regulation, in April 2014, Brazil issued the mandatory Resolution No. 4327, which requires regulated entities to set up and implement environmental and social risk policies along with an implementation action plan. The resolution covers credit, legal, and reputational risks that may arise from environmental and social issues (CBB 2014; Centre for Sustainability Studies 2014).

3.3.5   Europe

European banks were not exposed to the same liabilities as their US and Canadian counterparts and thus tended to focus more on the development of new environmental products than on risk assessment (Labatt and

White 2003). However, the European strategy for CSR defines CSR as "the responsibility of enterprises for their impacts on society". In order to fully meet their CSR, enterprises should have in place a process to integrate social, environmental, ethical, human rights, and consumer concerns into their business operations and core strategy in close collaboration with their stakeholders and with the aim of:

1. maximizing the creation of shared value for their owners/shareholders and for their other stakeholders and society at large and
2. identifying, preventing, and mitigating their possible adverse impacts (EC 2011).

Moreover, through Directive 2014/95/EU (that amends accounting directive 2013/34/EU), European Union (EU) law requires large companies to disclose certain information regarding the way they operate and manage social and environmental challenges. Under this Directive, large companies have to publish reports on the policies they implement in relation to environmental protection, social responsibility, and treatment of employees, respect for human rights, anticorruption and bribery, and diversity on company boards (in terms of age, gender, and educational and professional background) (EC 2014).

Currently, 27 EU member states have fully transposed the Directive with the exception of Spain. In June 2017, the European Commission published its own guidelines on environmental and social information disclosure. These guidelines are not mandatory, and companies may decide to use international, European, or national guidelines according to their own characteristics or business environment.

By transposing EC Directive 2014/95/EU, in 2016, the Italian government approved Legislative Decree No. 254/2016 calling for the disclosure of nonfinancial and diversity information. The decree sets out the requirement for public interest entities to draw up an annual nonfinancial statement containing information regarding the entity's development, performance, position, and the impact of the entity's operations on environmental, social, employment, human rights, anticorruption, and bribery matters. The new disclosure requirements apply to public interest entities, which are defined as Italian companies meeting both of the following criteria:

1. Categorized as one of the following: (i) issuers of securities traded on Italian or European regulated markets, (ii) banks, (iii) insurance companies, or (iv) reinsurance companies.
2. Exceeding, on an individual or consolidated basis, (i) 500 employees on average during the relevant fiscal year as well as (ii) at least one of the following thresholds: total net asset value of €20,000,000 or total net revenues from sales and services of €40,000,000 at the end of the relevant fiscal year.

3.3.6   China

In 2007, the China Banking Regulatory Commission (CBRC), the People's Bank of China (PBOC), and the Ministry of Environmental Protection (MEP) jointly issued the Green Credit Policy, which called on banks to consider environmental impact and energy efficiency as part of lending decisions (Wang and Bernell 2013). In particular, according to the Green Credit Policy, banks should restrict money loaned to companies with poor environmental performance (Jin and Mengqi 2011; Zhang et al. 2011).

Based on the Green Credit Policy, the PBoC published the Green Credit Guidelines demanding that banks put restrictions on loans to polluting industries and offer adjusted interest rates depending on the environmental performance of the borrowers' sectors (Zhao and Xu 2012; Weber 2016).

3.4   CSR and Sustainability: Interconnected Concepts

The expectations of stakeholders—and in general of community—regarding sustainable development have strengthened the importance of CSR practices in banks. However, the quality of this type of disclosure differs among countries and economic sectors. Banks tend to improve their CSR policies by setting action plans, objectives, and goals, and publishing dedicated reports.

More specifically, after the turmoil, an increasing number of banks voluntarily disclose information about the environmental and social impacts on society of their main activities (Wright 2012; Caldecott and

McDaniels 2014). A recent work (Laidroo and Sokolova 2015) regarding the CSR disclosure scores of international banks in 2013 observes that it was significantly larger than in 2005. However, the research also emphasizes that (1) significant improvements remained in the area of sustainable products and environmental management policies, and (2) although the transnational context had contributed to the gradual convergence of CSR disclosure scores, the existence of differing national and organizational contexts maintained some of the diversity across banks. Indeed, more and more banks increasingly admit their *"responsibility of indirect involvement in environmental damages and recognize their environmental sustainability which is one part of their Corporate Environmental Responsibility (CER) and Corporate Social Responsibility"* (Jo et al. 2015, p. 258). The disclosure quality of European banks is increased with the endorsement of IAS/IFRS principles, particularly regarding credit risk exposure (Bischof 2009). At the same time, voluntary standards for environmental risks and sustainable banking and finance are emerging (Fullwiler 2015). Therefore, recently, the sustainability communication process and sustainability disclosure in banks have become imperative, and risk management and reporting have primary responsibility.

Many works develop a quantitative methodological approach to explore how banks integrate sustainability criteria in credit risk assessment in German and Swiss banks (Weber et al. 2010), Canadian banks (Weber 2012), Bangladeshi banks (Weber et al. 2015), and Chinese banks (Weber 2016), while a few studies propose qualitative analysis to explore the phenomena (Weber 2012) or to compare the recent practices adopted by banks located in different geographical areas. As mentioned, despite the high quality of the extant research, this stream delves into largely unexplored terrain, and further investigations are required. In particular, relatively few studies address environmental risk management and reporting in the banking industry, and there are no studies that focus on banks located in the Euro area. More specifically, few studies focus on sustainability report disclosure in the banking sector, despite the interest shown by the financial sector toward CSR issues and sustainability/environmental risks related to the credit risk management criteria adopted (Carnevale and Mazzuca 2014).

Actually, at the international level, several key changes are occurring in the regulation and supervision of banking (and financial) systems, and sometimes, with regard to environmental risk management, the situation is different in different countries. However, regardless of the regulatory regime, several banks—in particular, large banks (Nelson et al. 2008)—have incentives to voluntarily provide information regarding their engagement with (and commitment to) environmental and social activities and sustainable practices (Carnevale and Mazzuca 2014).

3.5   EMERGING PRACTICES: ENVIRONMENTAL CREDIT RISK MANAGEMENT

The analysis of environmental credit risk management (ECRM) in banks can be useful for better understanding the linkages between finance and sustainability. From a theoretical viewpoint, a few works focus on environmental issues in the operation of banks and analyze how environmental risk can be integrated into the credit risk management process. More specifically, researchers have explored ECRM in banks, focusing on (1) how sustainability issues are integrated into credit risk assessment procedures in commercial lending (Thompson and Cowton 2004; Weber et al. 2010; Weber 2012; Weber and Banks 2012), (2) the positive relationship between sustainability performance and financial performance (Weber 2016), (3) the potential reputational damage arising from environmental-related issues (Campbell and Slack 2011), (4) the relevance of the environmental risk in lending decisions (Thompson and Cowton 2004; Weber 2012; Weber et al. 2015), and (5) the linkages between systemic environmental risk and bank sector stability (Alexander 2014).

The relationship between the financial sector and sustainable development is analyzed by Weber (2014) in three main aspects: (1) the influence that the sector may have through financed projects or borrowers, (2) the emerging risks connected with sustainability, and (3) the reputational risks that may arise from stakeholder pressure also in terms of financial performance.

As noted by Mengze and Wei (2015, p. 159) *"for most banks the primary basis for sustainable finance is incorporating environmental consideration into their bank lending products and services such as lending, project finance etc."* Many banks consider environmental risks as part of the credit appraisal process, and detailed guidelines for integrating environmental assessment into credit risk assessment have been published (Weber et al.

2008). Since the 1990s, environmental legislation has increased, and many banks have developed risk assessment procedures to offset potential liability for environmental damage caused by their borrowers in addition to developing many CSR and risk agendas (Coulson and O'Sullivan 2014). Banks have come to realize that banking operations, in particular lending, affect and are affected by the environment and that, consequently, they might have an important role in helping to raise environmental standards (Thompson 1998; Emtairah et al. 2005; Mengze and Wei 2015; Weber et al. 2015). Weber et al. (2015, p. 2) underline that some banks apply sustainability criteria to lending business to manage their risks, as well as to improve their reputation (Nandy and Lodh 2012). Several examples exist of banks that have improved their proactive environmental engagement (Weber 2012). After all, as stated by Weber (2012, p. 248) *"one of the main businesses of banks is the loan business, and thus credit risk management is a major activity to guarantee the business success of a bank. Those lenders that are best able to evaluate and price risks will be successful in the banking business (...). In order to be successful, lenders must rate those factors that influence the borrower's ability to repay the loan. (...) In theory, these factors are called counterparty credit risks and have a main influence on the default risk of a borrower."*

Environmental risks influence counterparty risk, and therefore, banks affect sustainable development both directly through their "day-to-day" operational activities (Iraldo et al. 2011) and indirectly through the products and services they offer (Thompson 1998; Case 1999; Weber 2012). From this perspective, it is clear that some financial regulators, international organizations and agencies have addressed the connection between sustainable development, environmental risks, and banking sector efficiency and stability (Weber and Feltmate 2016). But it is only after the crisis of 2007–2008 that the reform process of banking regulation has to consider the aim of generating *"sustainable and balanced global growth"* (G20 Summit Leaders' Statement 2009). Several initiatives worldwide are addressing this issue. In 2012, the IFC started gathering financial policy makers and regulators around sustainability issues via the Sustainable Banking Network. In 2014, the United Nations Environment Programme launched an inquiry into the alignment of the global financial system with long-term, sustainable development. The Basel II Framework (with Pillars II and III) has introduced an implementation of credit risk measurement and management, as well as the major disclosure of key information regarding banks' risk profile (Chernobai et al. 2008).[2] An interesting report by Alexander (2014) focuses on the implementation of Basel III and the financial stability risks associated with systemic environmental risks, analyzing the measures taken to modulate the prudential regulations that are applied to banks according to the environmental risk. According to this work, the regulation does not affect it, although there is evidence of a group of countries (including Brazil, China, and Peru) and their banking industries that have adopted regulatory and governance practices to deal with systemic environmental risks. The work also notes that the Basel Committee should learn more from experience and consider reforms to Pillar 2 (Supervisory Review framework) and Pillar 3 (Market Discipline framework), which would involve recognizing systemic environmental risks as risks that potentially threaten banking stability. Basel III has been criticized by a number of authors who argue that it could have problematic implications for the transition to a sustainable economy (Alexander 2014; Caldecott and McDaniels 2014).

3.6   Creating Value Through Sustainable Business Models

In the new and emerging movements that are increasing sustainability concerns around banking activities, many drivers may be detected. Muriithi and Louw (2017) underline that the major drivers toward sustainability within the banking industry are represented by the development of regulatory frameworks and guidelines aimed at making financial institutions responsible for their environmental and social impacts.

Moreover, bankers can make the identification of environmental risk a *positive* aspect of their service to and relationship with their customers (Case 1999, p. 13) as well as an essential component of the functioning and stability of the financial system. At the same time, an interesting report provided by the IFC in 2014—conducted in nine countries (Bangladesh, Brazil, Colombia, Indonesia, Nigeria, Peru, the Philippines, Thailand, and Vietnam) and involving 123 financial institutions—observed the potential benefits of environmental and social risk management. In particular, the survey highlights the following potential benefits: improvement of loan portfolio quality (28%), improved brand value (22%), attraction of investment (22%), new business opportunities (14%), and improved analyst ratings (9%) (IFC 2014).

Jeucken and Bouma (1999) categorize the driving forces for more proactive policies toward sustainable development by distinguishing between internal and external. Internal driving forces are likely to come from employees, shareholders, and the board of directors, while external driving forces result from pressures from governments, customers, competitors, nongovernmental organizations (NGOs), and society at large (the public).

Weber (2005) found five models for the successful integration of sustainability into the banking business: event-related integration of sustainability, sustainability as a new banking strategy, sustainability as a value driver, sustainability as a public mission, and sustainability as a requirement of clients.

Weber and Feltmate (2016, p. 46) highlight that there are 12 sustainability value drivers that can create business value. These drivers are: (1) customer attraction/retention, (2) employee satisfaction/retention/productivity, (3) evolving securities commission reporting requirements, (4) operational efficiency, (5) media pressure/exposure, (6) industry self-regulation, (7) inclusion in sustainability indexes and/or funds, (8) access to markets, (9) legal due diligence/insurance, (10) due diligence regarding partnerships/acquisitions, (11) discounted loan rates, and (12) facilitation of divestitures.

Moving from the consideration that most changes in the ways in which banks relate to sustainability will come from the outside—from society and governments, for example—rather than from the inside, the following sections provide an overview of the major driving forces toward sustainability within the banking industry (Fig. 3.1).

As described in Fig. 3.1, by grouping into homogeneous categories the suggestion provided by Weber and Feltmate (2016), four main driving forces may be highlighted. The fifth driving force is drawn from the suggestion of Jeucken and Bouma (1999).

3.6.1   Regulation and Legal Framework

At the international level, a number of countries have taken a strategic approach to harnessing the financial system both in the form of mandatory regulation and in the form of voluntary guidelines. Wagner and Schaltegger (2003) highlight that the purpose of environmental regulation is to correct for negative externalities.

External pressure is also represented by the NGOs which are calling for the implementation of more socially and environmentally friendly lending

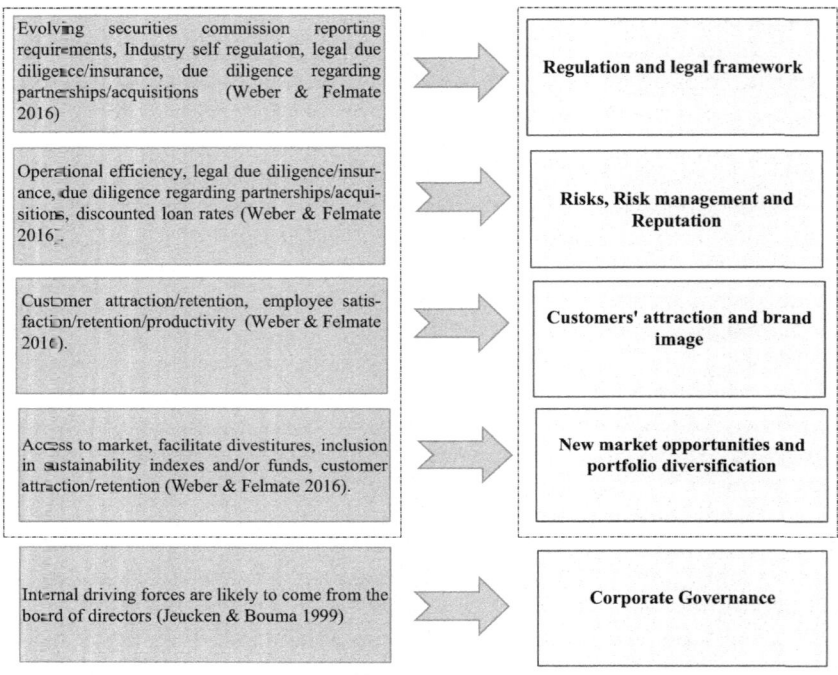

Fig. 3.1 Driving forces behind sustainability in banks (Source: our elaboration)

policies (e.g., UNEP FI and IFC). These NGOs and international bodies have the objective of influencing a bank's financial products and services to adhere to sustainability principles (Tan et al. 2017). The increasing pressure to comply with regulations imposed at the national or international level has forced the banking industry to do the following:

- Create new business products (e.g., green bonds and green funds).
- Introduce the environmental risk management process.
- Increase the level of disclosure.

By offering competitive financial products and services to customers, and by complying with rules and regulations, banks are able to gain competitive advantages as well as protect themselves from unmanaged or underestimated risks by ensuring financial stability, thus increasing performance.

3.6.2   Risk Management, Performance, and Reputation

The banking sector as a whole is less concerned about its direct environmental impact than with the implication for the direct impact of their customers' activities. In this sense, banks are more interested in appraising corporate environmental risk and performance when they lend or invest money (Lee et al. 2002); in terms of direct impact on the environment compared with other sectors such as oil and gas or transportation, the banking industry is generally perceived as a "clean sector" (Schmidheiny and Zorraquin 1998; Jeucken 2010; Viganò and Nicolai 2009; Bouma et al. 2017).

Thompson and Cowton (2004) argued that banks face three levels of risk associated with environmental exposure through lending: indirect, direct, and reputational risk.[3] Following this classification, Campbell and Slack (2011) clarify that indirect risks are related to the possibility of a borrower' inability to repay the capital sum due to the adverse financial consequences of changes in environmental regulation or changes in demand for its products due to environmental sentiment. On the contrary, direct risk refers to the possibility that the bank has taken over a security from a defaulting borrower and is now faced with the associated costs of environmental cleanup (Case 1999).

The risk management process is one of the major drivers for value creation (Schröck and Steiner 2005) (Fig. 3.2).

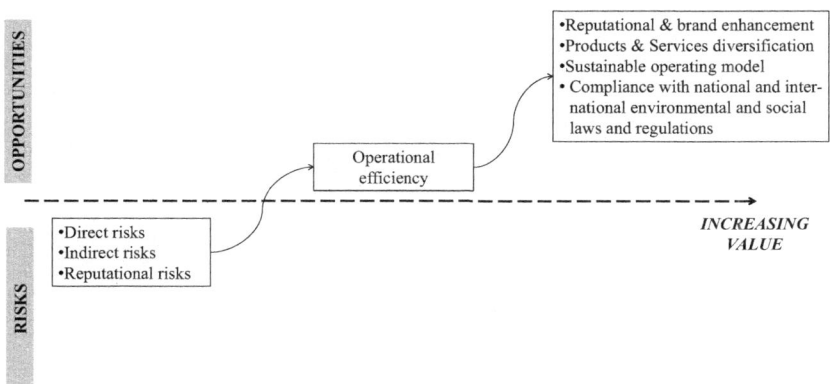

Fig. 3.2 From risk management activities to increased value (Source: our elaboration)

Generally, "*risk management is the systematic application of management policies, processes, and procedures to the tasks of identifying, analyzing, assessing, treating, and monitoring risk. The aim of the risk management process is to reduce exposure to the consequences of risk events to levels that are considered acceptable by the business*" (Bowden et al. 2001, p. 15). Risk management comprises a series of steps: (1) define the context and risk management criteria; (2) identify the risks; (3) assess the significance of those risks; (4) identify, select, and implement risk treatment options; and (5) perform monitoring, review, and corrective actions (Bowden et al. 2001, p. 8). However, the question is how risk management activities and process can be linked to the overall objective of value maximization.

Several works have focused on why risk management at the corporate level is necessary from a value creation perspective rather than how much or what kind of risk management practices and activities are optimal for banks (Froot and Stein 1998; Schröck and Steiner 2005). In this sense, Cebenoyan and Strahan (2004) highlight that the benefits of advances in risk management in banking may be greater credit availability rather than reduced risk in the banking system. Froot and Stein (1998) stressed the relation between risk management, capital budgeting, and capital structure policies for banks, while Schroeck (2002) argued that risk management can create value when it reduces costs.

Reputational risk is arguably the most significant of the environmental risks (Case 1999). The role of reputation is self-evident in the banking industry because this concept is related to the nature and function of banking business in the context of contemporary theories on financial intermediation (Trotta et al. 2016).

Banks can potentially fall victim to bad reputations if they finance projects that are seen as environmentally or socially problematic or if they do business with firms in trouble because of environmental or social problems (Weber et al. 2008).

In particular, Campbell and Slack (2011, p. 56) state that "*reputation risk is where the banks, though a lending decision, face a loss of reputation due to adverse environmental actions by the borrowing company. By providing loan finance, the bank may be seen as complicit in environmental damage and as such is exposed to potential adverse public reputational risk*".

Managing risks, in particular reputational risks, related to environmental issues undoubtedly represents one of the major drivers of value creation.

The potential impact of unmanaged environmental and social risks on reputation may be disruptive. Addressing environmental risks with responsibility means to carefully weigh the anticipated added value against possible hazards. Stringent risk management with precisely defined processes and a strict system of internal controls help to manage risks by avoiding the negative effects on stakeholders.

Finally, borrowers may be encouraged to adopt better management practices that will lead to an overall better environmental performance. This will be a particularly useful contribution for sustainable development.

3.6.3   Customers' Attraction and Brand Image

Customers are interested not only in the added value of a product or service but also the entire banking operations (Jeucken 2010). As stated by Matute-Vallejo et al. (2011, p. 317): *"In a world where consumer confidence in the banking industry has been bruised over the last few years, searching for solutions to rebuild trust and maintain clients' loyalty is a critical task not only for bank managers, but also for strategic management and marketing research"*. Being perceived as a powerful brand is a good way to reduce perceived risk-taking and obtain a sustainable competitive advantage (de Chernatony and Cottam 2006; O'Loughlin and Szmigin 2005; Kay 2006). Moreover, a strong corporate image may lead to loyalty on the part of consumers as well as investors and employees (Riordan et al. 1997; Andreassen and Lindestad 1998; Fombrun and Shanley 1990; Lemmink et al. 2003). The relationship between customers and sustainable banking may be explored from two others perspectives. First, customers are the first reason for banks to develop sustainable banking products. Finally, by recognizing the impact of their lending and investment operations, through their policies banks may influence the activities of customers.

3.6.4   New Market Opportunities and Portfolio Diversification

Increased concerns about environmental and sustainability themes have led to demands by customers for the development of specialized products and services and the systematic integration of climate change-related aspects into the core business processes of banks. Several international banks have recently adopted innovative, proactive strategies to capture the opportunities associated with sustainability. To this end, key initiatives (further described in the next chapters of this book) include green bonds, green funds, sustainable investment funds, and impact investing. The benefits obtained from environmental sustainability practices assist in product differentiation and/or cost reduction in addition to encouraging a resource-based view of the firm (Orsato 2006). According to Porritt (2001), these benefits can be grouped into five categories: eco-efficiency, quality management, license to operate, market advantage, and sustainable profits.

3.6.5   Corporate Governance

Financial scandals and financial misconduct continue to foster the debate over whether banks should include social elements as part of their corporate goals or focus exclusively on maximizing shareholder returns. The role of boards in corporate decision-making and on firm performance has been widely assessed in the academic literature (Westphal and Fredrickson 2001; Peng 2004; Kakabadse 2007; Post et al. 2011). Studies relating to CSR and corporate governance (CG) highlight a complex yet strong relationship between the two concepts (Sharma and Khanna 2014). However, over the last number of years, CG discussions have shifted progressively toward contemporary social issues (e.g., climate change, labor rights, and corruption) that matter to lawmakers, consumers, shareholders, and corporate managers (Walls et al. 2012).

Board members, through the formation of board committees, should address the concerns of sustainable development (Ricart et al. 2005). Consequently, CG can be viewed as a vehicle for incorporating social and environmental concerns into the business decision-making process, with positive effects not only for financial investors but also for employees, consumers, and communities.

3.7   Summary and Conclusions

This chapter highlighted the role of banks in sustainable development. At the same time, it described the reasons for the increased focus on sustainability and environmental issues. In this sense, banks are constantly pressured by numerous stakeholders to engage in social and environmental responsibility, and many regulatory and international frameworks have been developed. The driving forces behind sustainability have been detected, categorized, and discussed. Among them, risk management activities have the major role of protecting banks from environmental risks and related costs but, at the same time, they may represent a harmful instrument for creating new business opportunities. In particular, during the last years, new sustainable products and services have emerged such as green bonds, green funds, or sustainable development funds. The emergence of these new products represents a way for banks to improve their offerings, thereby attracting new customers, or diversify their portfolio by mitigating their risk exposure. Moreover, by incorporating sustainability principles into corporate strategy funding decisions and product/service definition processes, banks can be influential in supporting and promoting environmentally and/or socially responsible projects and enterprises. Banks actively engaged in sustainable or green practices—and perceived as such—may increase their reputation among customers, financial regulators, and the entire financial system.

By understanding the potentiality—in terms of value creation—of "being sustainable", banks are changing their *modus operandi*. However, two major aspects should be considered: banks are moving toward more sustainable business models because they are being forced by the changing regulatory landscape and because they are aware of the incredible market opportunities that sustainability represents.

NOTES

1. The principles are detailed as follows: Principle 1—Definition: Positive Impact Finance is that which serves to finance a positive impact. Business is that which serves to deliver a positive contribution to one or more of the three pillars of sustainable development (economic, environmental, and social), once any potential negative impacts on any of the pillars have been duly identified and mitigated. By virtue of this holistic appraisal of sustainability issues, Positive Impact Finance constitutes a direct response to the challenge of financing the Sustainable Development Goals (SDGs); Principle 2—Frameworks: to promote the delivery of Positive Impact Finance, entities (financial or nonfinancial) need adequate processes, methodologies, and tools to identify and monitor the positive impact of the activities, projects, programmers, and/or entities to be financed or invested in; Principle 3—Transparency: entities (financial or nonfinancial) providing Positive Impact Finance should provide transparency and disclosure on the following: (1) the activities, projects, programs, and/or entities financed that are considered positive impact and the intended positive impacts thereof (as per Principle 1); (2) the processes they have in place to determine eligibility and to monitor and to verify impacts (as per Principle 2); (3) the impacts achieved by the activities, projects, programs, and/or entities financed (as

per Principle 4); Principle 4—Assessment: the assessment of Positive Impact Finance delivered by entities (financial or nonfinancial) should be based on the actual impacts achieved. For further details, see UNEP FI (2017).

2. On the concept of risk culture in banks with an overview on the role of regulation, see Carretta et al. 2017.
3. On the subjects of banking reputation and reputational risk, see, among others, Fiordelisi et al. (2013, 2014), Dell'Atti and Trotta (2016), and Miklaszewska and Kil (2017). On the relationship between CSR and reputation in the banking industry, see Dell'Atti et al. (2017).

References

Alexander, K. (2014). *Stability and sustainability in banking reform: Are environmental risks missing in Basel III*. Cambridge/Geneva: CISL & UNEPFI.

Bischof, J. (2009). The effects of IFRS 7 adoption on bank disclosure in Europe. *Accounting in Europe, 6*(2), 167–194.

Bouma, J. J., Jeucken, M., & Klinkers, L. (Eds.). (2017). *Sustainable banking: The greening of finance*. New York: Routledge.

Bowden, A. R., Lane, M. R., & Martin, J. H. (2001). *Triple bottom line risk management: Enhancing profit, environmental performance, and community benefits*. New York: Wiley.

Caldecott, B., & McDaniels, J. (2014). *Financial dynamics of the environment: Risks, impacts, and barriers to resilience. Documento de trabajo del Estudio del PNUMA*. UNEP Inquiry/Smith School, Oxford University.

Campbell, D., & Slack, R. (2011). Environmental disclosure and environmental risk: Sceptical attitudes of UK sell-side bank analysts. *The British Accounting Review, 43*(1), 54–64.

Canadian Securities Administrators (CSA). (2010). *CSA Staff notice 51-333 – Environmental reporting guidance*. Retrieved November 6, 2017, from http://www.osc.gov.on.ca/documents/en/Securities-Category5/csa_20101027_51-333_environmental-reporting.pdf

Carnevale, C., & Mazzuca, M. (2014). Sustainability report and bank valuation: Evidence from European stock markets. *Business Ethics: A European Review, 23*(1), 69–90.

Carretta, A., Fiordelisi, F., & Schwizer, P. (2017). *Risk culture in banking*. Cham: Palgrave Macmillan.

Case, P. (1999). *Environmental risk management and corporate lending: A global perspective*. Cambridge: Woodhead Publishing.

Cebenoyan, A. S., & Strahan, P. E. (2004). Risk management, capital structure and lending at banks. *Journal of Banking & Finance, 28*(1), 19–43.

Central Bank of Brazil. (2014). *Resolution No. 4,327 on social and environmental responsibility for financial institutions*. Retrieved from http://www.bcb.gov.br/pre/normativos/res/2014/pdf/res_4327_v1_O.pdf

Centre for Sustainability Studies. (2014). *The Brazilian financial system and the green economy – Alignment with sustainable development.* Retrieved from http://unepinquiry.org/wp-content/uploads/2015/10/brazilianfinancial-systemgreeneconomy_febraban-gvces_april2015.pdf

Chapman, J., & Damar, H. E. (2015). International banking and liquidity risk transmission: Evidence from Canada. *IMF Economic Review, 63*(3), 455–478.

Chernobai, A. S., Rachev, S. T., & Fabozzi, F. J. (2008). *Operational risk: A guide to Basel II capital requirements, models, and analysis* (Vol. 180). Hoboken: Wiley.

Cooperman, E. S. (2016). *Managing financial institutions: Markets and sustainable finance.* Florence: Taylor & Francis.

Coulson, A., & O'Sullivan, N. (2014). Environmental and social assessment in finance. In J. Bebbington, J. Unerman, & B. O'Dwyer (Eds.), *Sustainability accounting and accountability.* London: Routledge.

De Chernatony, L., & Cottam, S. (2006). Why are all financial services brands not great? *Journal of Product & Brand Management, 15*(2), 88–97.

Dell'Atti, S., & Trotta, A. (2016). *Managing reputation in the banking industry. Theory and practice.* Switzerland: Springer.

Dell'Atti, S., Trotta, A., Iannuzzi, A. P., & Demaria, F. (2017). Corporate social responsibility engagement as a determinant of bank reputation: An empirical analysis. *Corporate Social Responsibility and Environmental Management, 24*(6), 589–605.

Emtairah, T., Hansson, L., & Guo, H. (2005). Environmental challenges and opportunities for banks in China: The case of industrial and commercial bank of China. *Greener Management International, 50,* 85.

European Commission. (2011). *A renewed EU strategy 2011–14 for Corporate Social Responsibility.* Retrieved November 6, 2017, from http://eur-lex.europa.eu/legal-content/EN/TXT/PDF/?uri=CELEX:52011DC0681&from=EN

European Commission. (2014). *Directive 2014/95/EU of the European Parliament and the Council of 22 October 2014 amending Directive 2013/34/EU as regards disclosure of non-financial and diversity information by certain large undertakings and groups.* Retrieved November 6, 2016, from http://eur-lex.europa.eu/legal-content/EN/TXT/PDF/?uri=CELEX:32014L0095&from=EN

Fiordelisi, F., Soana, M. G., & Schwizer, P. (2013). The determinants of reputational risk in the banking sector. *Journal of Banking & Finance, 37*(5), 1359–1371.

Fiordelisi, F., Soana, M. G., & Schwizer, P. (2014). Reputational losses and operational risk in banking. *The European Journal of Finance, 20*(2), 105–124.

Fombrun, C., & Shanley, M. (1990). What's in a name? Reputation building and corporate strategy. *Academy of Management Journal, 33*(2), 233–258.

Froot, K. A., & Stein, J. C. (1998). Risk management, capital budgeting, and capital structure policy for financial institutions: An integrated approach. *Journal of Financial Economics, 47*(1), 55–82.

Fullwiler, S. T. (2015). Sustainable finance: Building a more general theory of finance. *Binzagr Institute for Sustainable Prosperity* (Working Paper 106).

G20. (2009, September). *Leaders' statement Pittsburgh summit.* Retrieved from http://www.g20.utoronto.ca/2009/2009communique0925.html

Giddings, B., Hopwood, B., & O'brien, G. (2002). Environment, economy and society: Fitting them together into sustainable development. *Sustainable Development, 10*(4), 187–196.

Herzig, C., & Moon, J. (2013). Discourses on corporate social ir/responsibility in the financial sector. *Journal of Business Research, 66*(10), 1870–1880.

International Finance Corporation (IFC). (2007). *Banking on sustainability: Financing environmental and social opportunities in emerging markets.* Washington, DC: International Finance Corporation (IFC).

International Finance Corporation (IFC). (2014). *Moving forward with environmental and social risk management.* Washington, DC: International Finance Corporation. Retrieved from https://www.ifc.org/wps/wcm/connect/3a10 98804316ae1fb602fe384c61d9f7/ESRM-Report-Final.pdf?MOD=AJPERES

Iraldo, F., Melis, M., & Sabbatino, A. (2011). *Environmental strategies by the banking sector: Case studies in the Italian context.* Retrieved from https://papers.ssrn.com/sol3/papers.cfm?abstract_id=1761962

Jeucken, M. (2010). *Sustainable finance and banking: The financial sector and the future of the planet.* London: Routledge.

Jeucken, M. H., & Bouma, J. J. (1999). The changing environment of banks. *Greener Management International, 27*, 21–21.

Jin, D., & Mengqi, N. (2011). The paradox of green credit in China. *Energy Procedia, 5*, 1979–1986.

Jo, H., Kim, H., & Park, K. (2015). Corporate environmental responsibility and firm performance in the financial services sector. *Journal of Business Ethics, 131*(2), 257–284.

Kakabadse, A. P. (2007). Being responsible: Boards are reexamining the bottom line. *Leadership in Action, 27*(1), 3–6.

Kay, M. J. (2006). Strong brands and corporate brands. *European Journal of Marketing, 40*(7/8), 742–760.

Labatt, S., & White, R. R. (2003). *Environmental finance: A guide to environmental risk assessment and financial products* (Vol. 200). Hoboken: Wiley.

Laidroo, L., & Sokolova, M. (2015). International banks' CSR disclosures after the 2008 crisis. *Baltic Journal of Management, 10*(3), 270–294.

Lee, B. W., Jung, S. T., & Chun, Y. O. (2002). Environmental accounting in Korea: Cases and policy recommendations. In M. Bennett & J. J. Bouma (Eds.), *Environmental management accounting: Informational and institutional developments. Eco-efficiency in industry and science* (Vol. 9, pp. 175–186). Dordrecht: Springer.

Lehner, O. M. (Ed.). (2016). *Routledge handbook of social and sustainable finance.* Abingdon/New York: Routledge.

Lemmink, J., Schuijf, A., & Streukens, S. (2003). The role of corporate image and company employment image in explaining application intentions. *Journal of Economic Psychology, 24*(1), 1–15.

Liu, S. (2012). Improving financial stability: Can European Union member states learn from China's experience in enhancing commercial banks' social responsibilities? *European Law Journal, 18*(1), 108–121.

Matute-Vallejo, J., Bravo, R., & Pina, J. M. (2011). The influence of corporate social responsibility and price fairness on customer behaviour: Evidence from the financial sector. *Corporate Social Responsibility and Environmental Management, 18*(6), 317–331.

Mengze, H., & Wei, L. (2015). A comparative study on environment credit risk management of commercial banks in the Asia-Pacific region. *Business Strategy and the Environment, 24*(3), 159–174.

Miklaszewska, E., & Kil, K. (2017). Reputational risk in banking: Important to whom? In G. Chesini, E. Giaretta, & A. Paltrinieri (Eds.), *The business of banking* (Palgrave Macmillan Studies in Banking and Financial Institutions, pp. 109–129). Cham: Palgrave Macmillan.

Muriithi, S. M., & Louw, L. (2017). The Kenyan banking industry: Challenges and sustainability. In A. Ahmed (Eds.), *Managing knowledge and innovation for business sustainability in Africa* (Palgrave Studies of Sustainable Business in Africa, pp. 197–222). Cham: Palgrave Macmillan.

Nandy, M., & Lodh, S. (2012). Do banks value the eco-friendliness of firms in their corporate lending decision? Some empirical evidence. *International Review of Financial Analysis, 25*, 83–93.

Nelson, B., Wohlmannstetter, G., Ferron-Jolys, M. C., & Labuschagne, R. (2008). *Focus on transparency-Trends in the presentation of financial statements and disclosure of information by European banks.* London: KPMG.

O'Loughlin, D., & Szmigin, I. (2005). Customer perspectives on the role and importance of branding in Irish retail financial services. *International Journal of Bank Marketing, 23*(1), 8–27.

Orsato, R. (2006). Competitive environmental strategies: When does it pay to be green? *California Management Review, 48*(2), 127–143.

Peng, M. W. (2004). Outside directors and firm performance during institutional transitions. *Strategic Management Journal, 25*, 453–471.

Pichler, K., & Lehner, O. (2017). European Commission – New regulations concerning environmental and social impact reporting. *ACRN Oxford Journal of Finance and Risk Perspectives, 6*(1), 1–54.

Porritt, J. (2001). *The world in context: Beyond the business case for sustainable development.* Cambridge: University of Cambridge Programme for Industry.

Post, C., Rahman, N., & Rubow, E. (2011). Green governance: Boards of directors' composition and environmental corporate social responsibility. *Business & Society, 50*(1), 189–223.

Ricart, E. J., Rodríguez, A. M., & Sánchez, P. (2005). Sustainability in the board-room: An empirical examination of Dow Jones sustainability world index leaders. *Corporate Governance: The International Journal of Business in Society, 5*(3), 24–41.

Riordan, C. M., Gatewood, R. D., & Bill, J. B. (1997). Corporate image: Employee reactions and implications for managing corporate social perfor-mance. *Journal of Business Ethics, 16*(4), 401–412.

Rybczynski, T. M. (1997). A new look at the evolution of the financial system. In ~. Revell (Ed.), (2016). *The recent evolution of financial systems* (pp. 3–15). Basingstoke: Springer, Palgrave Macmillan UK.

Santomero, A. M. (1984). Modeling the banking firm: A survey. *Journal of Money, Credit and Banking, 16*(4), 576–602.

Saunders, A., & Cornett, M. M. (2013). *Financial institutions management: A risk management approach.* New York: Irwin/McGraw-Hill.

Schaltegger, S., Burritt, R., & Petersen, H. (2017). *An introduction to corporate environmental management: Striving for sustainability.* New York: Routledge.

Schmidheiny, S., & Zorraquin, F. J. (1998). *Financing change: The financial com-munity, eco-efficiency, and sustainable development.* Cambridge: MIT press.

Scholtens, B. (2009). Corporate social responsibility in the international banking industry. *Journal of Business Ethics, 86*(2), 159–175.

Schroeck, G. (2002). *Risk management and value creation in financial institutions* (Vol. 155). Hoboken: Wiley.

Schröck, G., & Steiner, M. (2005). Risk management and value creation in banks. In M. Frenkel, M. Rudolf, & U. Hommel (Eds.), *Risk management.* Berlin/Heidelberg: Springer.

Sharma, J. P., & Khanna, S. (2014). Corporate social responsibility, corporate gov-ernance and sustainability: Synergies and inter-relationships. *Indian Journal of Corporate Governance, 7*(1), 14–38.

Shiller, R. J. (2013). *Finance and the good society.* Princeton: Princeton University Press.

Strandberg, C. (2005). *Best practices in sustainable finance.* Strandberg Consulting. Retrieved from http://www.social-banking.org/fileadmin/isb/Artikel_und_Studien/Strandberg_Sustainable_Finance_Best_Practices.pdf

Swiss Finance Initiative. (2016). *What is sustainable finance?* Retrieved from http://sfi.ch/node/3080

Tan, L. H., Tan, L. H., Chew, B. C., Chew, B. C., Hamid, S. R., & Hamid, S. R. (2017). A holistic perspective on sustainable banking operating system drivers: A case study of Maybank group. *Qualitative Research in Financial Markets, 9*(3), 240–262.

Thompson, P. (1998). Assessing the environmental risk exposure of UK banks. *International Journal of Bank Marketing, 16*(3), 129–139.

Thompson, P., & Cowton, C. J. (2004). Bringing the environment into bank lending: Implications for environmental reporting. *The British Accounting Review, 36*(2), 197–218.

Trotta, A., Iannuzzi, A. P., & Pacelli, V. (2016). Reputation, reputational risk and reputational crisis in the banking industry: State of the art and concepts for improvements. In S. Dell'Atti & A. Trotta (Eds.), *Managing reputation in the banking industry* (pp. 3–22). Cham: Springer.

UNEP FI. (2015). *UNEP FI Positive Impact Manifesto.* http://www.unepfi.org/fileadmin/documents/PositiveImpactManifesto.pdf. Last accessed Nov 2017.

UNEP FI. (2017). *UNEP FI statement.* http://www.unepfi.org/about/unep-fi-statement/. Last accessed Nov 2017.

Viganò, F., & Nicolai, D. (2009). CSR in the European banking sector: Evidence from a survey. In *Corporate social responsibility in Europe: Rhetoric and realities* (pp. 95–108). Cheltenham: Edward Elgar Publishing.

Wagner, M., & Schaltegger, S. (2003). How does sustainability performance relate to and business competitiveness? *Greener Management International, 44*, 5–16.

Wallin Andreassen, T., & Lindestad, B. (1998). Customer loyalty and complex services: The impact of corporate image on quality, customer satisfaction and loyalty for customers with varying degrees of service expertise. *International Journal of Service Industry Management, 9*(1), 7–23.

Walls, J. L., Berrone, P., & Phan, P. H. (2012). Corporate governance and environmental performance: Is there really a link? *Strategic Management Journal, 33*(8), 885–913.

Wang, H., & Bernell, D. (2013). Environmental disclosure in China: An examination of the green securities policy. *The Journal of Environment & Development, 22*(4), 339–369.

Weber, O. (2005). Sustainability benchmarking of European banks and financial service organizations. *Corporate Social Responsibility and Environmental Management, 12*(2), 73–87.

Weber, O. (2012). Environmental credit risk management in banks and financial service institutions. *Business Strategy and the Environment, 21*(4), 248–263.

Weber, O. (2014). The financial sector's impact on sustainable development. *Journal of Sustainable Finance & Investment, 4*(1), 1–8.

Weber, O. (2016). *The sustainability performance of Chinese banks: Institutional impact.* Retrieved from https://papers.ssrn.com/sol3/papers.cfm?abstract_id=2752439

Weber, O., & Banks, Y. (2012). Corporate sustainability assessment in financing the extractive sector. *Journal of Sustainable Finance & Investment, 2*(1), 64–81.

Weber, O., & Feltmate, B. (2016). *Sustainable banking: Managing the social and environmental impact of financial institutions.* Toronto: University of Toronto Press.

Weber, O., & Remer, S. (Eds.). (2011). *Social banks and the future of sustainable finance.* Oxon/New York: Taylor & Francis.

Weber, O., Fenchel, M., & Scholz, R. W. (2008). Empirical analysis of the integration of environmental risks into the credit risk management process of European banks. *Business Strategy and the Environment, 17*(3), 149–159.

Weber, O., Scholz, R. W., & Michalik, G. (2010). Incorporating sustainability criteria into credit risk management. *Business Strategy and the Environment, 19*(1), 39–50.

Weber, O., Hoque, A., & Ayub Islam, M. (2015). Incorporating environmental criteria into credit risk management in Bangladeshi banks. *Journal of Sustainable Finance & Investment, 5*(1–2), 1–15.

Westphal, J. D., & Fredrickson, J. W. (2001). Who directs strategic change? Director experience, the selection of new CEOs, and change in corporate strategy. *Strategic Management Journal, 22*, 1113–1137.

Wheeler, S. M. (2013). *Planning for sustainability: Creating livable, equitable and ecological communities.* London: Routledge.

White, A. L. (2006). *The stakeholder fiduciary: CSR, governance and the future of boards.* San Francisco: Business for Social Responsibility.

Wright, C. (2012). Global banks, the environment, and human rights: The impact of the equator principles on lending policies and practices. *Global Environmental Politics, 12*(1), 56–77.

Yüksel, Ü. (Ed.). (2016). *Sustainability and management: An international perspective.* London/New York: Taylor & Francis.

Zhang, B., Yang, Y., & Bi, J. (2011). Tracking the implementation of green credit policy in China: Top-down perspective and bottom-up reform. *Journal of Environmental Management, 92*(4), 1321–1327.

Zhao, N., & Xu, X.-j. (2012). Analysis on green credit in China. *Advances in Applied Economics and Finance (AAEF), 3*(21), 501–506.

CHAPTER 4

Emerging Practices in Sustainable Banking

Abstract Environmental concerns are pushing banks toward the development of new products, investment, and communication strategies. From the banks' point of view, sustainable products may be seen as both a strategic and a commercial opportunity. At the same time, communicating the bank engagement in sustainable approaches may represent a pathway toward new market opportunities in terms of reputation and customer perception. This chapter gives an overview of the most important sustainable products and services developed by the banking industry and describes the role of sustainability disclosure in terms of both opportunities and risks of inactions.

Keywords Sustainable banking • Green bonds • Disclosure

4.1 Introduction

From the banks' perspective, the issues related to sustainable development have an important strategic and commercial dimension. In addition to risk management tools, traditional commercial banks have developed new products that both encourage improved environmental performance on the customers' side and provide environmental businesses with easier access to capital (Labatt and White 2011; Bouma et al. 2017). The threats and opportunities for banks that arise out of the sustainable development

© The Author(s) 2018
R. Carè, *Sustainable Banking*,
https://doi.org/10.1007/978-3-319-73389-0_4

can be divided into several categories by a range of criteria: from risk reduction to profit generation and from purely business to ideological reasons (Jeucken 2010).

The banking sector intermediates financial flows by borrowing funds from individual depositors or a wide range of organizations and channeling these financial resources to individual and corporate borrowers, mainly in the form of business and commercial lending. Consequently, by developing or providing sustainable banking products, they play a triple role. First, they provide financial resources, and in some cases financial advice, to new sustainable projects or initiatives by promoting the diffusion of a form of "sustainable business thinking". Second, they may support nongovernmental organizations (NGOs) and governments in the development of new sustainable policies. Third, they may improve their market share, reputation, and image by being perceived as sustainable and committed banks.

At the same time, being a sustainable bank involves not only providing products and services but also offering a different approach in terms of transparency and communication.

Nonfinancial disclosure—including sustainability and environmental disclosure—represents the main tools to communicate the banks' commitments toward sustainability.

This chapter gives an overview of the most important sustainable products and services developed by the banking industry and describes the role of sustainability disclosure in terms of both risks and opportunities. The main reasons for sustainable banking products and services are synthetized in Sect. 4.2, while the main sustainable financial products/services are summarized in Sect. 4.3. Then, Sects. 4.4 and 4.5 recognize the role of sustainability disclosure and the main voluntary approaches that have been developed in recent years.

4.2   SUSTAINABLE BANKING PRODUCTS AND SERVICES: REASONS AND MOTIVATIONS

Environmental concerns in general, and issues regarding climate change in particular, are pushing banks toward the development of new products and investment strategies. From the banking perspective, sustainable development has a commercial dimension (Jeucken 2010). Financial capitals are considered as the most important ingredients in supporting a sustainable development (Weber and Feltmate 2016), and in recent years, sustainable investment practices have experienced an exceptional growth by representing the bridge between an unsustainable present and a sustainable future (Robins 2008). In this sense, banks play a key role in channeling funds to firms that seek financing to implement business projects, and consequently, the banks can monitor and push firms to operate in an eco-friendly or socially responsible way by imposing restrictions or requirements tailored to improve the environment or society (Chen et al. 2017). Pursuing innovative financial solutions and products generates direct profits in new markets with new clients. All these elements contribute to improving the bank's brand value (IFC 2007).

Figure 4.1 summarizes the main opportunities and risks that banks may face in the development (or in the nondevelopment) of products and services related to the issue of sustainable development.

As highlighted in Fig. 4.1, reputational considerations represent the most important trigger for the development of sustainable banking products. Benefits for banks in improving new sustainable banking products range from increased profitability and market value to a stronger reputation and improved image in the community.

4.3   The Commercial Dimension of Sustainability: Products and Services

Sustainable financial products and services are highly variable depending on the region, level of development, market and industry structure, and consumer/client preferences (UNEP FI 2016). The popularity and acceptance of these new sustainable financial products in the capital markets have also risen due to the investor demand for such investments, and these products are available to wholesale and retail investors (Anderson 2015). During the last years, banks have introduced particular products that meet the needs of their clients through the introduction of payment, savings, and investment products and by serving as financial intermediaries, thus creating products such as environmental loans and leases (Labatt and White 2003).

In addition, financial institutions have become involved in the securitization of projects that are in the early stages of development. Finally, banks have developed advisory products and services that assist companies with

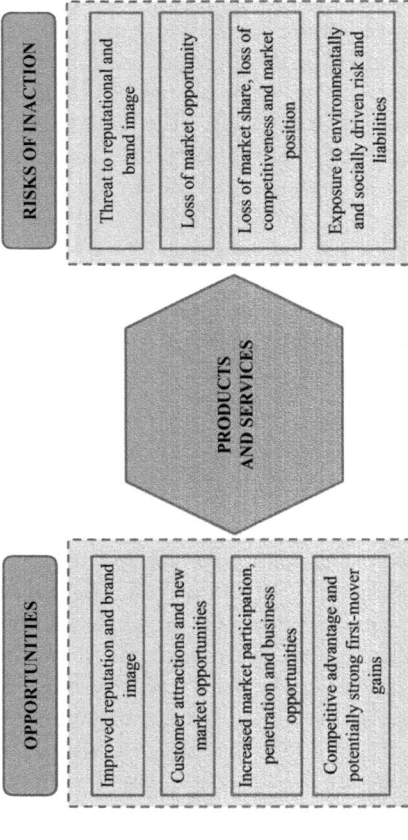

Fig. 4.1 Opportunities and risks of inactions in developing sustainable banking products and services (Source: Our elaboration)

Table 4.1   Examples of sustainable banking products

Business line	Products
Retail banking	Home mortgages
	Commercial building loan
	Home equity loan
	Affinity card
	Green credit cards
	Technology leasing
	Microcredit and microfinance
Corporate and investment banking	Project finance
	Partial credit guarantees
	Securitization
	Green, social, sustainable, and/or positive impact bonds
	Indices
	Private equity and venture capital
	Carbon finance and emissions trading
	Weather derivatives
	Debt-for-nature swaps
Asset management	Green fiscal funds
	Funds (e.g., carbon funds, clean energy targeted fund)
	Impact investing funds
Insurance	Environmental damage insurance.
	Bank guarantees environmental risks
Consultancy	SME environmental plan

Source: Our elaboration. SME: small- and medium-sized enterprise

their environmental risk management (Jeucken 2010). Examples of sustainable banking products are summarized in Table 4.1.

The following sections describe the most important sustainable banking products.

4.3.1   Home Mortgages, Commercial Building Loans, and Home Equity Loans

Green mortgages provide lower interest rates than market rates, and homes provided or upgraded with these mortgages are more energy efficient and have more energy efficient appliances. Similarly, banks can also choose to provide green mortgages by covering the cost of switching a house from conventional to green power and include this consumer benefit when marketing the product (UNEP FI 2007). The delivery of green mortgage products takes on different formats at different financial institutions (Labatt and White 2003). Home equity loans are designed and offered in order to motivate households to install residential renewable energy (power or thermal) technologies. In designing and offering these incentive-based products, a number of banks have also partnered with technology providers and environmental NGOs (UNEP FI 2007).

4.3.2   *Affinity Cards and Green Credit Cards*

Green and affinity credit cards are offered by most large credit card companies, which typically offer NGO donations equal to approximately half a percentage point on every purchase, balance transfer or cash advance made by the card owner. Donations are made to each of the partnered NGOs from income generated by the use of the credit cards (Labatt and White 2003). The commercial benefits for banks are visible in an enhanced image and better sales of other products, particularly to young people, and it is thus a form of "cause-related marketing" (Jeucken 2010).

4.3.3   *Microcredit and Microfinance[1]*

Microfinance has emerged as a tool to offer financial services to poor customers (La Torre and Vento 2008; Armendáriz and Morduch 2010; Armendáriz and Szafarz 2011; Hudon 2009). The European Union (EU) promotes microcredit as an important strategy to support small businesses and, at the same time, is also committed to protecting the environment (Forcella and Hudon 2016). Banks are increasingly interested in offering micro loans to individuals and small and medium-sized enterprises (SMEs), which are generally denied credit (public or private), in order to finance small environmental projects, such as small solar installations (UNEP FI 2007). Currently, Credit Suisse, Société Genérale, and Santander have entered this area.

4.3.4   *Leasing and Renting*

Banks are increasingly developing forms of environmental leasing in which they provide environmentally friendly technologies at preferential rates to commercial customers. In this sense, in 2015, Santander Group closed more than 300 finance transactions for upward of €35 million to fund numerous LED lighting, boiler exchange, waste treatment projects, and so on. It also has 1037 solar photovoltaic array lease finance arrangements totaling €245 million (Santander Sustainability Report 2017).

4.3.5   Green Bonds

Green bonds are innovative financial instruments in which the proceeds are invested exclusively (by specifying the use of the proceeds, direct project exposure, or securitization) in green projects that generate climate or other environmental benefits (such as renewable energy, energy efficiency, sustainable waste management, biodiversity, clean transportation, and clean water). In recent years, more countries joined the green bond market (such as France, Norway, Canada, and Poland), contributing to a total annual issuance of US$41.8 billion. Corporate green bonds accounted for 36% of the issuance—the highest share ever, followed by municipalities with 15% and by banks with 12% (EC 2016; OECD 2017). The first world's green bond—named the Climate Awareness Bond (CAB)—was launched in 2007 by the European Investment Bank[2] (EIB) (Galaz et al. 2015; Flaherty et al. 2017). As clarified in the Green Bond Principles (GBP),[3] four different types of green bonds currently exist in the market (ICMA 2017, p. 6):

- Standard Green Use of Proceeds Bond: a standard recourse-to-the-issuer debt obligation aligned with the GBP;
- Green Revenue Bond: a nonrecourse-to-the-issuer debt obligation aligned with the GBP in which the credit exposure in the bond is to the pledged cash flows of the revenue streams, fees, taxes, and so on, and whose use of proceeds goes to related or unrelated Green Project(s);
- Green Project Bond: a project bond for single or multiple Green Project(s) in which the investor has direct exposure to the risk of the project(s) with or without potential recourse to the issuer and that is aligned with the GBP;
- Green Securitized Bond: a bond collateralized by one or more specific Green Project(s), including, but not limited to, covered bonds, asset-backed securities (ABS), mortgage-backed securities (MBS), and other structures, and is aligned with the GBP. The first source of repayment is generally the cash flows of the assets.

The guidelines provided by the GBP helped the market to grow quickly. Traditional commercial banks are increasingly selling green bonds of their own while also bulking up their role as underwriters in helping other borrowers market their debt to investors. In 2013, Bank of America issued the first benchmark-sized corporate green bond—a $500 million offering—and also coauthored the GBP. During the last years, *Bank of America Merrill Lynch (BofAML)* issued a total of $2.1 billion in three separate offerings, including a $1 billion offering in November 2016, and in 2016, underwrote more than $25 billion in green bonds on behalf of 27 unique clients. According to Bloomberg New Energy Finance, BofAML was the top underwriter of green bonds in 2014, 2015, and 2016 and led offerings for clients, such as the Chinese automobile company Zhejiang Geely Holdings ($400 million), the New York Metropolitan Transportation

Table 4.2   Top financial issuers in 2016 ($ billions)

Bank	Country	Total amount
Top financial issuers		
Shanagi Pudong Development Bank	China	7.59
Industrial Bank	China	7.41
Bank of Communications	China	4.36
Bank of China	China	3.68
Bank of Qingdao	China	1.19
Bank of America Merrill Lynch	USA	1.00
Jiangxi Bank	China	0.75
Berlin Hyp	Germany	0.56
Société Générale	France	0.56
ABN Amro	Netherlands	0.56
Top green bond underwriters		
Bank of America Merrill Lynch	USA	$7825m
Crédit Agricole	France	$4624m
JPMorgan	USA	$4264m
SEB Bank	Sweden	$3763m
Bank of China	China	$3653m
Morgan Stanley	USA	$3628m
Deutsche Bank	German	$3128m
Guotai Junan Securities Co Ltd	China	$3104m
HSBC	UK	$2818m
China Construction Bank	China	$2474m
Citigroup	USA	$2473m
Huatai Securities Co Ltd	China	$2457m
Barclays	UK	$2084m
China International Capital Cor	China	$2047m
Haitong Securities Co Ltd	China	$1965m

Source: Bloomberg New Energy Finance (2016)

Authority, and the EIB (five bonds in 2016 totaling $3.6 billion) (BofAML 2017, p. 9). Table 4.2 shows the top financial issuers and underwriters of green bonds in 2016.

4.3.6   Green Bond Funds and Green Bond Indices

Another way for investing in green bonds is via green bond funds[4] (Anderson 2015), while green bond indices[5] identify specific bonds as green via a stated methodology and allow investors to invest in a portfolio of green bonds to diversify risks. To this extent, the green bond index providers also effectively act as institutions of certification. Currently, global green bond indices are provided by Bank of America Merrill Lynch, Barclays MSCI, Standard & Poor's, and Solactive (Anderson 2015; Ehlers and Packer 2017)

4.3.7   Securitization

Securitization is the process of transforming a pool of illiquid assets (e.g., mortgages) into tradable financial instruments (e.g., securities) (Shenker and Colletta 1990).[6] A recent deal from Crédit Agricole showed the potential for synthetic securitization to free up regulatory capital for green investments. According to the Organisation for Economic Co-operation and Development (OECD), in Europe, green ABS annual issuance could reach US$84 billion by 2035 (37% of green securities) (OECD 2016). Globally, the annual issuance of green ABS for renewable energy, energy efficiency, and low-emission vehicles (LEVs) could reach between US$280 and US$380 billion by 2035 (OECD 2016).

4.3.8   Debt-for-Nature Swaps

Debt-for-nature swaps are financial transactions in which a portion of a government's or private sector entity's foreign debt is forgiven in exchange for local investments in environmental conservation measures (Dalal et al. 2015). Despite the fact that the swaps were attractive, they did not provide a profit for the investor, but they provided an avenue for banks to remove high-risk claims from their books and to promote the protection of forest ecosystems (Dalal et al. 2015). The idea behind this particular kind of financial instrument is that the loan, listed far below its nominal value, is entirely written off, or can be bought back by the debtor for far less than its nominal value, with the stipulation that the debtor spends the relief in his or her own country in an environmentally friendly way (Jeucken 2010). Debt-for-nature swaps are considered as the starting point for the development of a number of new approaches for long-term financing for conservation (Resor 1997). In the last years, many commercial banks (e.g., JP Morgan, Citibank, Bank of Tokyo, and Deutsche Bank) have been involved in such swaps (Jeucken 2010).

4.3.9   Green Fiscal Funds

Green fiscal funds had been launched by the Dutch government in 1992–1993 in collaboration with the banking sector (in particular ASN Bank and Triodos Bank) and differ from sustainable investment funds due to the attractive fiscal advantages they offer the investors and the green nature of the project (whereas sustainable investment funds focus solely on companies) (Jeucken 2010).

4.3.10   Impact Investment Funds

Impact investment funds are established with a specific mission and aim that are pursued through an investment strategy (Chiappini 2017). For the investor, the structure of an impact fund is often similar to a traditional private equity fund (Stagars 2015). In 2017, Barclays announced the launch of its multi-impact growth fund, offering retail and institutional investors the opportunity to generate long-term capital growth while the bank emphasizes making a positive contribution to society. The multi-impact growth fund invests primarily in specialist third-party funds that have been identified by Barclays' fund and a manager selection team. These funds have been selected as best-in-class based on both their potential for strong financial returns and the consideration of their impact around key social and environmental issues.[7]

4.4   Transparency and Communication in Sustainable Banking: Nonfinancial Disclosure

Nonfinancial disclosure has been steadily increasing in both size and complexity over the last years. In the academic literature, a variety of terms have been coined in order to define such organizational accounting and disclosure practices that fall beyond the financial domain: "social and environmental", "corporate social responsibility" (CSR), "sustainability", "ethical", and "triple bottom line" (Skouloudis et al. 2014). The investor community is showing a growing interest in such information for a more precise valuation of the firm (Berthelot et al. 2012; Sullivan and Gouldson 2012), and, at the same time, the phenomenon of corporate social and environmental disclosure has attracted research attention (Gray et al. 2001). CSR or sustainability disclosure can be defined as the set of information that a company discloses about "its environmental impact and its relationship with its stakeholders by means of relevant communication channels" (Campbell 2004; Gray et al. 2001; Gamerschlag et al. 2011). In contrast to financial reporting, corporate environmental disclosure is industry specific, voluntary, and discretionary, and this kind of information is of interest to many stakeholders (e.g., regulators, governments, and community groups) (Aerts et al. 2006; Barbu et al. 2014; D'amico et al. 2016). Many theoretical attempts have been made to explain how and why companies voluntarily disclose CSR information (Dowling and Pfeffer 1975; Gray et al. 1995b; Gamerschlag et al. 2011). In this sense, Aerts et al. (2006) highlight that according to institutional theory, firms respond to contextual pressures by following a general accepted way of doing business to appear legitimate to investors and stakeholders. Jain et al. (2015) classify the incentives for voluntary disclosure into two main categories: those that are based on economic drivers and those based on strategic motives. In particular, Cormier and Magnan (2003) highlight that an environmental reporting strategy is determined by (1) benefits from a reduction in information asymmetry and in the overall information gathering costs to be assumed by investors (information costs), (2) costs resulting from the disclosure of proprietary information, and (3) environmental media visibility (p. 47). Cormier and Magnan (2007) investigate the impact of environmental reporting on the relationship between a firm's earnings and its stock market value, and their results show that the interaction between environmental reporting, financial statement information, and firm stock market value is conditioned by the reporting context of firms.[8] The academic literature typically emphasizes the association between corporate environmental performance and corporate environmental reporting by using sociopolitical and economics-based theories of disclosure to explain variation in disclosures (Hahn and Kühnen 2013; Hahn et al. 2015; Braam et al. 2016). Sociopolitical theories of disclosure, including legitimacy theory, explain that corporate reporting issues cannot be investigated if considerations about the political, social, and institutional framework in which accounting activities occur and the conflicting interests of societal groups are disregarded (Gray et al. 1995a; Braam et al. 2016).

To date, only few studies explore the sustainability disclosure status in the banking sector (Khan et al. 2009; Khan 2010; Carnevale and Mazzuca 2014; Nobanee and Ellili 2016).

4.5   The Relationship Between Environmental Disclosure, Environmental Performance, and Firm Performance

After the financial crisis, banks have changed their approach to CSR and especially to CSR disclosure, being more aware of the potential reputational risks and brand image damage related to these issues (Scholtens 2006; Thompson and Cowton 2004; Carnevale and Mazzuca 2014). Sustainability reporting can positively affect the stakeholders' perceptions of firm performance, value, risk, profitability, share price and cost of capital (Gray et al. 1995b; Scholtens 2008; Cormier et al. 2011; Jizi et al. 2014). Miles and Covin (2000) examine the relationship between environmental performance, reputation and financial performance by concluding that being a good environmental steward provides firms with a reputational advantage that leads to enhanced financial performance. Similarly, Konar and Cohen (2001) highlight that poor environmental performance has significant negative effects on reputation. By analyzing the interrelations between environmental disclosure, environmental performance, and economic performance, Al-Tuwaijri et al. (2004) highlight a positive relationship and that "good" environmental performance is significantly associated with "good" economic performance. The quality and quantity of sustainability and thus voluntary disclosure in the banking sector is highly variable and is strictly influenced by a series of aspects. As clarified by the European Commission (EC 2017), appropriate nonfinancial disclosure is an essential element to enable sustainable finance. In suggesting what may be considered as Key Performance Indicators (KPIs), the recent guidelines on nonfinancial reporting from the EC (2017/C 215/01)[9] state: "*A bank may consider that its own water consumption in offices and branches is not a material issue to be included in its management report. In contrast, the bank may assess that the social and environmental impacts of projects that it funds and its role in supporting the real economy of a city, a region or a country are material information*" (EC 2017, p. 6).[10] Figure 4.2 summarizes the main risks and opportunities that may arise from the decision to disclose or not to disclose nonfinancial information.

4.6   VOLUNTARY CODE OF CONDUCTS

Since the 2000s, the higher public awareness of global warming has pushed financial institutions to take up efforts to combat climate change and social transformations, and be socially responsible by adopting voluntary codes of conduct. A code of conduct, also referred to as a "codes of ethics" or "codes of business standards", is designed to explicitly detail an organization's commitment to CSR. In particular, codes of conduct are a practical CSR instrument commonly used to govern employee behavior and establish a socially responsible organizational culture (Erwin 2011). Despite their voluntary and informal nature, firms may still interpret them as a set of obligations that need to be met in order to respond to public expectations and prevent damages to corporate reputation (Wright and Rwabizambuga 2006). Previous works that have analyzed the effectiveness of these codes have been widely discussed and empirically tested (Erwin 2011). Further, adopting codes of conduct may lead to reputational benefits by functioning as a symbol of CSR awareness and engagement, thereby preserving and legitimating the public image (Matten 2003). Numerous studies have investigated the content of codes (Jenkins 2001; Gaumnitz and Lere 2004) by showing that these reports are primarily descriptive. As stated by Richardson (2005), codes of conduct are innovative and important instruments for the promotion of fundamental human, labor and environmental rights, and anticorruption practices, especially in countries where public authorities fail to enforce minimum standards, but it should be underlined that they are complementary to national and international legislation and are not a substitute for them.

Major providers of sustainability reporting guidance and voluntary code of conducts also include: Global Reporting Initiative (GRI's Sustainability Reporting Standards), the OECD (OECD Guidelines for Multinational Enterprises), the United Nations (UN) Global Compact, and the International Organization for Standardization (ISO 26000, International Standard for social responsibility). A series of works has been carried out with a view to analyze the reasons for their great acceptance, both in academic literature (see among others: Richardson 2005;

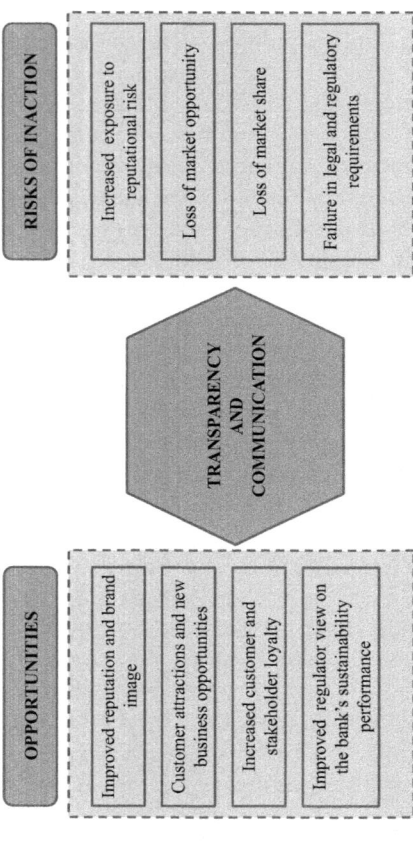

Fig. 4.2 Opportunities and risks of inaction related to disclosure (Source: Our elaboration)

Van der Laan 2009; Arevalo et al. 2013; Moratis and Brandt 2017) and in practitioner literature (McKinsey and Company 2007). In particular, some of these works have tried to analyze the reasons that have led firms to adopt this initiative (Bennie et al. 2007; Janney et al. 2009; Simone Byrd 2009) by concluding that the main reasons are to improve corporate reputation and image (Runhaar and Lafferty 2009). However, no clear consensus regarding the driving forces behind their adoption can be retrieved (Garayar et al. 2016).

4.6.1   Equator Principles

The equator principles (EPs) are a voluntary code of conduct and a risk management framework, adopted by equator principle financial institutions (EPFIs) for determining, assessing and managing environmental and the social risk associated with project finance initiatives (Chen et al. 2017).

The EPs have grown rapidly in terms of membership, geographic scope, and the requirements they impose on EPFIs and are now considered a "project finance industry standard" (Meyerstein, in Karen). Currently, 91 EPFIs in 37 countries have adopted the EPs.

The EPs apply to four financial products:

1. Project finance advisory services, where the total project capital costs are US$10 million or more
2. Project finance with total project capital costs of US$10 million or more
3. Project-related corporate loans (including export finance in the form of Buyer Credit) in which all four of the following criteria are met:
   (i)   The majority of the loan is related to a single project, over which the client has effective operational control (either direct or indirect).
   (ii) The total aggregate loan amount is at least US$100 million.
   (iii) The EPFI's individual commitment (before syndication or sell down) is at least US$50 million.
   (iv) The loan tenor is at least two years.
4. Bridge loans with a tenor of less than two years that are intended to be refinanced by project finance or a project-related corporate loan that is anticipated to meet the relevant criteria described above (EP 2013, p. 3).

The ten EPs span all phases of the project finance lending cycle and aim to fill the gaps between the national regulations and the International Finance Corporation's performance standards (Meyerstein 2015).

4.6.2   The Global Reporting Initiatives

The GRI is the most widely adopted sustainability reporting framework around the globe (KPMG 2017). The GRI network—in partnership with UN Environment Programme (UNEP)—includes the active participation of companies, entrepreneurs' associations, NGOs, workers' associations, government representatives, consulting firms, rating agencies, associations of chartered accountants, and auditing firms. The sustainability reporting guidelines are a framework for reporting on economic, environmental, and social performance that (1) outlines reporting principles and content to help prepare sustainability reports; (2) helps companies to gain a balanced picture of their economic, environmental, and social performance; (3) promotes comparability of sustainability reports; and (4) supports the assessment and benchmarking of sustainability performance (Adams and McNicholas 2007; Golob and Bartlett 2007; Khan et al. 2011). As a framework, the GRI considers that sustainability reporting can be "parallel" to financial reporting (compulsory in nature) by suggesting that the two reports together can enrich each other. The framework is built around the concept of the triple bottom line (Norman and MacDonald 2004; Finch 2015) and has a modular approach. In particular, the three universal standards (GRI 101, GRI 102, and GRI 103) are used by every organization that prepares a sustainability report, while topic-specific standards are used by organizations to report on material topics (economic, environmental, or social). The GRI Financial Services Sector Disclosures (GRI FSSD) document contains a set of disclosures for use by all organizations in the financial services sector. The disclosures cover key aspects of sustainability performance that are meaningful and relevant to the financial services sector and are not sufficiently covered in the G4 Guidelines. This sector supplement was issued in 2008 and developed based on the G3 Guidelines (2006). Following the launch of the G4 Guidelines in May 2013, the complete Sector Supplement content is now presented in the "Financial Services Sector Disclosures" document, in a new format, to facilitate its use in combination with the G4 Guidelines. It includes the original GRI Guidelines, which set out the reporting principles, disclosures on management approach and performance indicators for economic, environmental, and social issues, and which supplement additional commentaries and performance indicators developed especially for the sector and capture the issues that matter most for companies in the financial services sector (GRI, G4 Sector Disclosure—Financial Sector 2017). The level of compliance with the GRI recommendations is calculated according to whether the report addresses all the indicators or explains why any are omitted. Moreover, in order to achieve higher scores, companies can apply additional indicators that may improve their rating. Reports are rated C, C+, B, B+, A, or A+, with A+ being the highest rating given for businesses that fulfill all the GRI recommendations (Fuente et al. 2017).

4.6.3   *The International Standard for Social Responsibility: ISO 26000*

ISO is an independent, nongovernmental international organization with a membership of 162 national standards bodies. The standard was launched in 2010, following five years of negotiations between many different stakeholders across the world. ISO 26000 provides guidance on how businesses and organizations can operate in an ethical and transparent way that contributes to sustainable development while taking into account the expectations of stakeholders, applicable laws, and international norms of behavior (ISO 2016). The International Standard ISO 26000 provides harmonized, globally relevant guidance for private and public sector organizations of all types and encourages the implementation of worldwide best practices in social responsibility. ISO 26000 is a guidance standard that can be used by organizations on a voluntary basis (Sully 2012) and focuses on seven core subjects: *governance, human rights, labor, environment, business practices, consumers,* and *community* (Herciu 2016). In particular, ISO 26000 covers a wide range of sustainability issues and is not suitable for certification purposes which makes this standard different from other well-known standards (e.g., ISO 14001 or SA8000) (Hahn 2013). The standard outlines content and approaches to social responsibility and underlines that "social responsibility should be an integral part of core organizational strategy" (ISO 2010, p. 7).

4.6.4   The UN Global Compact

In 2000, the UN launched the UN Global Compact as a call to companies to align their operations and strategies with ten universally accepted principles in the areas of human rights, labor, environment, and anticorruption (UN 2017). The UN Global Compact is a strategic policy initiative that encourages businesses to support ten universal principles in the areas of human rights, labor standards, the environment, and anticorruption (Rasche and Kell 2010). The principles are derived from the Universal Declaration of Human Rights, the International Labour Organization's Declaration on Fundamental Principles and Rights at Work, UN Convention Against Corruption, and the Rio Declaration on Environment and Development (UN 2017). Unlike other multistakeholder schemes aimed at certification or reporting (GRI), the UN Global Compact is a principle-based initiative asking participants to align their operations and value chain activities with ten universally accepted principles (Rasche and Kell 2010). As of November 2017, 9.727 companies from 162 countries adopted the principles into their business practices and are taking actions to advance UN goals. In September 2015, all 193 member states of the UN adopted a plan for achieving a better future for all, over the next 15 years. At the heart of "Agenda 2030" are the 17 sustainable development goals (SDGs). The UN Global Compact's ten principles are the foundation for any company seeking to advance the SDGs (UN 2017).[11]

4.7   Conclusion

This chapter highlighted the main directions banks are moving toward in order to be sustainable. The first section summarized the opportunities and risks of inaction related to sustainable products and services. Reputational concerns are the most important trigger for the improvement of new products and services, followed by the opportunities to enter into new markets or to increase the market share by acquiring new customers. New banking products have emerged in recent time and span over all the banking branches and activities. Some products are emerging in the market for environmental or sustainable products, such as the impact investing funds, while others are being consolidated, such as affinity cards or green bonds. In particular, the latter represents one of the most important products for banks, which is confirmed by the increased attention and by the increased number of issuers and underwriters among banks all over the world. Additionally, sustainable services are emerging. Banks are starting to provide their consulting services to private business, as in the case of advisory services in green projects and initiatives. Then, the chapter moved toward the role of disclosure. Nonfinancial disclosure, including sustainability or environmental disclosure, is increasingly important for banks. This could be due to the bad image assigned by society to banks in the aftermath of the crisis. In recent years, many works tried to explore the role of nonfinancial disclosure from a firm perspective. However, it is not possible to identify univocal results. Undoubtedly, there is a strong relationship between a good reputation and a good disclosure. Moreover, the disclosed documents are often based on voluntary frameworks and initiatives. Banks are engaged in many programs and are trying to move their communication in order to communicate the sense of their sustainability and of their sustainability approach.

NOTES

1. For an overview of microcredit, microfinance, and microcredit guarantee funds, see, among others, Leone and Porretta (2014) and, La Torre and Vento (2008). For information on green microfinance, see: (Forcella 2013), Allet (2014), and Allet and Hudon (2015).
2. At the end of 2016, EIB was the world's largest issuer of Green Bonds with €15 billion raised.
3. The Green Bond Principles (GBP) have been updated in June 2017 and are voluntary process guidelines that recommend transparency and disclosure and promote integrity in the development of the Green Bond market, by clarifying the approach for issuance of a Green Bond.
4. On the topic of green bond funds' performance, see, among others, Scholtens (2011), Chang et al. (2012), and Adamo et al. (2014).
5. Indices are a primary investment tool for investment managers and investment owners, as they provide a benchmark or point of reference for the active investment decisions (Inderst et al. 2012).
6. About securitization, see Greenbaum and Thakor (1987), Ashcraft and Schuermann (2008), Maddaloni and Peydró (2011), and Mazzuca (2015).
7. For further details about impact investing, see Vecchi et al. (2015), Rizzello et al. (2016), Weber (2016), and Vecchi et al. (2017), while for more details on impact investment funds, see Stagars (2015) and Chiappini (2017).
8. Many academic works tried to explore the relationship between corporate environmental performance and firm performance. In this vein, Hassel

et al. (2005) show that environmental performance has a negative effect on the market value of a Swedish sample of firms. Murray et al. (2006), however, analyzed the value relevance of social and environmental reporting in UK companies, with no conclusive results. Different results are often attributed to the broad range or research methods and to the lack of common environmental performance measures (Konar and Cohen 2001; Al-Tuwaijri et al. 2004). Despite the growing number of works, mixed results have been found and the debate about the relationship between environmental performance and firm performance is still unresolved (Elsayed and Paton 2005; Lee et al. 2016; Nor et al. 2016).

9. The Directive 2014/95/EU of the European Parliament and of the Council (on disclosure of nonfinancial and diversity information by certain large undertakings and groups ("the Directive")) entered into force on 6 December 2014 and amends Directive 2013/34/EU (on the annual financial statements, consolidated statements and related reports of certain types of undertakings). Companies concerned will start applying the directive as of 2018, on information relating to the 2017 financial year. The disclosure requirements for nonfinancial information apply to certain large companies with more than 500 employees, as the cost of obliging SMEs to apply them could outweigh the benefits. Companies are required to disclose relevant, useful information that is necessary to understand their development, performance, position and the impact of their activity, rather than an exhaustive, detailed report. The directive also gives companies significant flexibility to disclose relevant information in the way that they consider most useful, including in a separate report. Companies may rely on international, EU-based, or national frameworks.

10. The EC decided on 28 October 2016 to establish a High Level Expert Group on sustainable finance. This builds on the Commission's goal to develop an overarching and comprehensive EU strategy on sustainable finance as part of the Capital Markets Union.

11. The Global Compact asks companies to embrace, support, and enact, within their sphere of influence, a set of core values in the areas of human rights, labor standards, the environment, and anticorruption. The principles are organized around four main areas: human rights (principles 1 and 2), labor standards (principles 3–6), environment (principles 7–9), and anticorruption (principle 10). The principles are as follows: Principle 1: Businesses should support and respect the protection of internationally proclaimed human rights; Principle 2: Make sure that they are not complicit in human rights abuses; Principle 3: Businesses should uphold the freedom of association and the effective recognition of the right to collective bargaining; Principle 4: The elimination of all forms of forced and compulsory labor; Principle 5: The effective abolition of child labor;

Principle 6: The elimination of discrimination in respect to employment and occupation; Principle 7: Businesses should support a precautionary approach to environmental challenges; Principle 8: Undertake initiatives to promote greater environmental responsibility; Principle 9: encourage the development and diffusion of environmentally friendly technologies; Principle 10: Businesses should work against corruption in all its forms, including extortion and bribery.

References

Adamo, R., Federico, D., & Notte, A. (2014). Performance and risk of green funds. *Investment Management and Financial Innovation, 11*(1), 134–145.

Adams, C. A., & McNicholas, P. (2007). Making a difference: Sustainability reporting, accountability and organisational change. *Accounting, Auditing & Accountability Journal, 20*(3), 382–402.

Aerts, W., Cormier, D., & Magnan, M. (2006). Intra-industry imitation in corporate environmental reporting: An international perspective. *Journal of Accounting and Public Policy, 25*(3), 299–331.

Allet, M. (2014). Why do microfinance institutions go green? *Journal of Business Ethics, 122*(3), 405–424.

Allet, M., & Hudon, M. (2015). Green microfinance: Characteristics of microfinance institutions involved in environmental management. *Journal of Business Ethics, 126*(3), 395–414.

Al-Tuwaijri, S. A., Christensen, T. E., & Hughes, K. E. (2004). The relations among environmental disclosure, environmental performance, and economic performance: A simultaneous equations approach. *Accounting, Organizations and Society, 29*(5), 447–471.

Anderson, J. (2015). Environmental finance. In *Handbook of environmental and sustainable finance* (pp. 307–333). Amsterdam: Academic Press.

Arevalo, J. A., Aravind, D., Ayuso, S., & Roca, M. (2013). The global compact: An analysis of the motivations of adoption in the Spanish context. *Business Ethics: A European Review, 22*(1), 1–15.

Armendáriz, B., & Morduch, J. (2010). *The economics of microfinance.* Cambridge, MA: MIT Press.

Armendáriz, B., & Szafarz, A. (2011). On mission drift in microfinance institutions. In B. Armendáriz & M. Labie (Eds.), *The handbook of microfinance* (pp. 341–366). London/Singapore: World Scientific Publishing.

Ashcraft, A. B., & Schuermann, T. (2008). Understanding the securitization of subprime mortgage credit. *Foundations and Trends® in Finance, 2*(3), 191–309.

Bank of America Merrill Lynch. (2017). *Bank of America corporation 2016 annual report*. Retrieved from https://about.bankofamerica.com/assets/pdf/BOAML_AR2016.pdf#page=11

Barou, E. M., Dumontier, P., Feleagă, N., & Feleagă, L. (2014). Mandatory environmental disclosures by companies complying with IASs/IFRSs: The cases of France, Germany, and the UK. *The International Journal of Accounting, 49*(2), 231–247.

Bennie, L., Bernhagen, P., & Mitchell, N. J. (2007). The logic of transnational action: The good corporation and the Global Compact. *Political Studies, 55*(4), 733–753.

Berthelot, S., Coulmont, M., & Serret, V. (2012). Do investors value sustainability reports? A Canadian study. *Corporate Social Responsibility and Environmental Management, 19*(6), 355–363.

Bloomberg New Energy Finance. (2016). *Clean energy investment trends, 2016*. New York.

Bouma, J. J., Jeucken, M., & Klinkers, L. (Eds.). (2017). *Sustainable banking: The greening of finance*. New York: Routledge.

Braam, G. J., de Weerd, L. U., Hauck, M., & Huijbregts, M. A. (2016). Determinants of corporate environmental reporting: The importance of environmental performance and assurance. *Journal of Cleaner Production, 129*, 724–734.

Campbell, D. (2004). A longitudinal and cross-sectional analysis of environmental disclosure in UK companies – A research note. *The British Accounting Review, 36*(1), 107–117.

Carnevale, C., & Mazzuca, M. (2014). Sustainability report and bank valuation: Evidence from European stock markets. *Business Ethics: A European Review, 23*(1), 69–90.

Chang, C. E., Nelson, W. A., & Doug Witte, H. (2012). Do green mutual funds perform well? *Management Research Review, 35*(8), 693–708.

Chen, N., Huang, H. H., & Lin, C. H. (2017). Equator principles and bank liquidity. *International Review of Economics & Finance*.

Chiappini, H. (2017). *Social impact funds: Definition, assessment and performance*. Cham: Springer.

Cormier, D., & Magnan, M. (2003). Environmental reporting management: A continental European perspective. *Journal of Accounting and Public Policy, 22*(1), 43–62.

Cormier, D., & Magnan, M. (2007). The revisited contribution of environmental reporting to investors' valuation of a firm's earnings: An international perspective. *Ecological Economics, 62*(3), 613–626.

Cormier, D., Ledoux, M. J., & Magnan, M. (2011). The informational contribution of social and environmental disclosures for investors. *Management Decision, 49*(8), 1276–1304.

D'Amico, E., Coluccia, D., Fontana, S., & Solimene, S. (2016). Factors influencing corporate environmental disclosure. *Business Strategy and the Environment, 25*(3), 178–192.

Dalal, S. P., Bonham, C., & Silvani, A. (2015). An investigation on ecosystem services, the role of investment banks, and investment products to foster conservation. In K. Wendt (Ed.), *Responsible investment banking. CSR, sustainability, ethics & governance.* Cham: Springer.

Dowling, J., & Pfeffer, J. (1975). Organizational legitimacy: Social values and organizational behavior. *Pacific Sociological Review, 18*(1), 122–136.

Ehlers, T., & Packer, F. (2017, September). Green bond finance and certification. *BIS Quarterly Review.* Retrieved from https://papers.ssrn.com/sol3/papers.cfm?abstract_id=3042378

Elsayed, K., & Paton, D. (2005). The impact of environmental performance on firm performance: Static and dynamic panel data evidence. *Structural Change and Economic Dynamics, 16*(3), 395–412.

Equator Principles. (2013). *The equator principles III.* The Equator Principles Assocaition, United Kingdom. Retrieved from http://www.equator-principles.com/resources/equator_principles_iii.pdf

Erwin, P. M. (2011). Corporate codes of conduct: The effects of code content and quality on ethical performance. *Journal of Business Ethics, 99*(4), 535–548.

European Commission. (2016). *Study on the potential of green bond finance for resource-efficient investments.* Retrieved from http://ec.europa.eu/environment/enveco/pdf/potential-green-bond.pdf

European Commission. (2017). *Guidelines on non-financial reporting (methodology for reporting non-financial information).* Communication from the commission 2017/C 215/01. Retrieved from http://eur-lex.europa.eu/legal-content/EN/TXT/PDF/?uri=CELEX:52017XC0705(01)&from=EN

Finch, N. (2015). Development of sustainability reporting frameworks: The case of Australia. In *Corporate social responsibility and governance* (pp. 227–239). Switzerland: Springer International Publishing.

Flaherty, M., Gevorkyan, A., Radpour, S., & Semmler, W. (2017). Financing climate policies through climate bonds–A three stage model and empirics. *Research in International Business and Finance, 42*, 468–479.

Forcella, D. (2013). *European green microfinance, a first look* (EMN research paper). Brussels.

Forcella, D., & Hudon, M. (2016). Green microfinance in Europe. *Journal of Business Ethics, 135*(3), 445–459.

Fuente, J. A., García-Sánchez, I. M., & Lozano, M. B. (2017). The role of the board of directors in the adoption of GRI guidelines for the disclosure of CSR information. *Journal of Cleaner Production, 141*, 737–750.

Galaz, V., Gars, J., Moberg, F., Nykvist, B., & Repinski, C. (2015). Why ecologists should care about financial markets. *Trends in Ecology & Evolution, 30*(10), 571–580.

Gameschlag, R., Möller, K., & Verbeeten, F. (2011). Determinants of voluntary CSR disclosure: Empirical evidence from Germany. *Review of Managerial Science, 5*(2–3), 233–262.

Garayar, A., Heras-Saizarbitoria, I., & Boiral, O. (2016). Adoption of the UN Global Compact in Spanish banking: A case study. *Journal of Public Affairs, 16*(4), 359–367.

Gaumnitz, B. R., & Lere, J. C. (2004). A classification scheme for codes of business ethics. *Journal of Business Ethics, 49*(4), 329–335.

Global Reporting Initiative. (2006). *G3 guidelines.* Amsterdam.

Global Reporting Initiatives. (2017). *G4 sector disclosure – Financial sector.* London.

Golob, U., & Bartlett, J. L. (2007). Communicating about corporate social responsibility: A comparative study of CSR reporting in Australia and Slovenia. *Public Relations Review, 33*(1), 1–9.

Gray, R., Kouhy, R., & Lavers, S. (1995a). Constructing a research database of social and environmental reporting by UK companies. *Accounting, Auditing & Accountability Journal, 8*(2), 78–101.

Gray, R., Kouhy, R., & Lavers, S. (1995b). Corporate social and environmental reporting: A review of the literature and a longitudinal study of UK disclosure. *Accounting, Auditing & Accountability Journal, 8*(2), 47–77.

Gray, R., Javad, M., Power, D. M., & Sinclair, C. D. (2001). Social and environmental disclosure and corporate characteristics: A research note and extension. *Journal of Business Finance & Accounting, 28*(3–4), 327–356.

Greenbaum, S. I., & Thakor, A. V. (1987). Bank funding modes: Securitization versus deposits. *Journal of Banking & Finance, 11*(3), 379–401.

Hahn, R. (2013). ISO 26000 and the standardization of strategic management processes for sustainability and corporate social responsibility. *Business Strategy and the Environment, 22*(7), 442–455.

Hahn, R., & Kühnen, M. (2013). Determinants of sustainability reporting: A review of results, trends, theory, and opportunities in an expanding field of research. *Journal of Cleaner Production, 59*, 5–21.

Hahn, R., Reimsbach, D., & Schiemann, F. (2015). Organizations, climate change, and transparency: Reviewing the literature on carbon disclosure. *Organization & Environment, 28*(1), 80–102.

Hassel, L., Nilsson, H., & Nyquist, S. (2005). The value relevance of environmental performance. *European Accounting Review, 14*(1), 41–61.

Herciu, M. (2016). ISO 26000 – An integrative approach of corporate social responsibility. *Studies in Business and Economics, 11*(1), 73–79.

Hudon, M. (2009). Should access to credit be a right? *Journal of Business Ethics, 84*, 17–28.

Inderst, G., Kaminker, C., & Stewart, F. (2012). *Defining and measuring green investments: Implications for institutional investors' asset allocations* (OECD working papers on finance, insurance and private pensions, no. 24). Paris: OECD Publishing.

International Capital Market Association. (2017). *The Green Bond Principles (GBP) 2017*. Retrieved from https://www.icmagroup.org/assets/documents/Regulatory/Green-Bonds/GreenBondsBrochure-JUNE2017.pdf

International Finance Corporation (IFC). (2007). *Banking on sustainability: Financing environmental and social opportunities in emerging markets*. Washington, DC: International Finance Corporation (IFC).

International Organization for Standardization. (2010). *Project overview*. Geneve: International Organization for Standardization.

International Organization for Standardization. (2016). *ISO and SDGS*. Geneve: International Organization for Standardization.

Jain, A., Keneley, M., & Thomson, D. (2015). Voluntary CSR disclosure works! Evidence from Asia-Pacific banks. *Social Responsibility Journal, 11*(1), 2–18.

Janney, J. J., Dess, G., & Forlani, V. (2009). Glass houses? Market reactions to firms joining the UN global compact. *Journal of Business Ethics, 90*(3), 407–423.

Jenkins, R. (2001). *Corporate codes of conduct: Self-regulation in a global economy* (Technology, Business and Society, Programme Paper Number 2). New York: UN Research Institute for Social Development.

Jeucken, M. (2010). *Sustainable finance and banking: The financial sector and the future of the planet*. Sterling: Routledge.

Jizi, M. I., Salama, A., Dixon, R., & Stratling, R. (2014). Corporate governance and corporate social responsibility disclosure: Evidence from the US banking sector. *Journal of Business Ethics, 125*(4), 601–615.

Khan, H. U. Z. (2010). The effect of corporate governance elements on corporate social responsibility (CSR) reporting: Empirical evidence from private commercial banks of Bangladesh. *International Journal of Law and Management, 52*(2), 82–109.

Khan, H. U. Z., Halabi, A. K., & Samy, M. (2009). Corporate social responsibility (CSR) reporting: A study of selected banking companies in Bangladesh. *Social Responsibility Journal, 5*(3), 344–357.

Khan, H. U. Z., Azizul Islam, M., Kayeser Fatima, J., & Ahmed, K. (2011). Corporate sustainability reporting of major commercial banks in line with GRI: Bangladesh evidence. *Social Responsibility Journal, 7*(3), 347–362.

Konar, S., & Cohen, M. A. (2001). Does the market value environmental performance? *The Review of Economics and Statistics, 83*(2), 281–289.

KPMG. (2017). *The KPMG survey of corporate responsibility reporting 2017*. New York: KPMG Global Sustainability Services.

La Torre, M., & Vento, G. (2008). Banks in the microfinance market. In *Frontiers of banks in a global economy* (Vol. 131). London: Palgrave Macmillan.

Labatt, S., & White, R. R. (2003). *Environmental finance: A guide to environmental risk assessment and financial products.* New York: Wiley.

Labatt, S., & White, R. R. (2011). *Carbon finance: The financial implications of climate change* (Vol. 362). Hoboken: Wiley.

Lee, K. H., Cin, B. C., & Lee, E. Y. (2016). Environmental responsibility and firm performance: The application of an environmental, social and governance model. *Business Strategy and the Environment, 25*(1), 40–53.

Leone, P., & Porretta, P. (2014). *Microcredit guarantee funds in the mediterranean: A comparative analysis.* New York: Palgrave Macmillan.

Maddaloni, A., & Peydró, J. L. (2011). Bank risk-taking, securitization, supervision, and low interest rates: Evidence from the Euro-area and the US lending standards. *The Review of Financial Studies, 24*(6), 2121–2165.

Matten, D. (2003). Symbolic politics in environmental regulation: Corporate strategic responses. *Business Strategy and the Environment, 12*(4), 215–226.

Mazzuca, M. (2015). *Cartolarizzazioni bancarie in Italia: nuove frontiere dopo la crisi.* Milan: EGEA spa.

McKinsey & Company. (2007). *UN Global Compact CEO participant survey.* New York: McKinsey.

Meyerstein, A. (2015). Are the equator principles greenwash or game changers? Effectiveness, transparency and future challenges. In *Responsible investment banking* (pp. 267–284). Cham: Springer International Publishing.

Miles, M. P., & Covin, J. G. (2000). Environmental marketing: A source of reputational, competitive, and financial advantage. *Journal of Business Ethics, 23*(3), 299–311.

Moratis, L., & Brandt, S. (2017). Corporate stakeholder responsiveness? Exploring the state and quality of GRI-based stakeholder engagement disclosures of European firms. *Corporate Social Responsibility and Environmental Management, 24*(4), 312–325.

Murray, A., Sinclair, D., Power, D., & Gray, R. (2006). Do financial markets care about social and environmental disclosure? Further evidence and exploration from the UK. *Accounting, Auditing & Accountability Journal, 19*(2), 228–255.

Nobanee, H., & Ellili, N. (2016). Corporate sustainability disclosure in annual reports: Evidence from UAE banks: Islamic versus conventional. *Renewable and Sustainable Energy Reviews, 55,* 1336–1341.

Nor, N. M., Bahari, N. A. S., Adnan, N. A., Kamal, S. M. Q. A. S., & Ali, I. M. (2016). The effects of environmental disclosure on financial performance in Malaysia. *Procedia Economics and Finance, 35,* 117–126.

Norman, W., & MacDonald, C. (2004). Getting to the bottom of "triple bottom line". *Business Ethics Quarterly, 14*(2), 243–262.

OECD. (2016). *A quantitative framework for analysing potential bond contributions in a low-carbon transition.* Retrieved from https://www.oecd.org/cgfi/quantitative-framework-bond-contributions-in-a-low-carbon-transition.pdf

OECD. (2017). *Mobilising bond markets for a low-carbon transition.* Retrieved from http://www.oecd.org/environment/cc/Green%20bonds%20PP%20[f3]%20[lr].pdf

Rasche, A., & Kell, G. (Eds.). (2010). *The United Nations global compact: Achievements, trends and challenges.* Cambridge: Cambridge University Press.

Resor, J. P. (1997). Debt-for-nature swaps: A decade of experience and new directions for the future. *Unasylva (FAO), 48*(188), 15–22.

Richardson, B. J. (2005). Equator principles: The voluntary approach to environmentally sustainable finance. *The European Environmental Law Review, 14,* 280.

Rizzello, A., Caré, R., Migliazza, M. C., & Trotta, A. (2016). Social impact investing: A model and research agenda. In O. Lehner (Ed.), *Routledge handbook of social and sustainable finance.* New York: Routledge.

Robins, N. (2008). The emergence of sustainable investing. In *Sustainable investing: The art of long-term performance* (pp. 3–18). London/Sterling: Earthscan.

Runhaar, H., & Lafferty, H. (2009). Governing corporate social responsibility: An assessment of the contribution of the UN Global Compact to CSR strategies in the telecommunications industry. *Journal of Business Ethics, 84*(4), 479–495.

Santander. (2017). *2016 sustainability report.* Madrid.

Scholtens, B. (2006). Finance as a driver of corporate social responsibility. *Journal of Business Ethics, 68*(1), 19–33.

Scholtens, B. (2008). A note on the interaction between corporate social responsibility and financial performance. *Ecological Economics, 68*(1), 46–55.

Scholtens, B. (2011, August). The sustainability of green funds. In *Natural resources forum* (Vol. 35, No. 3, pp. 223–232). Oxford: Blackwell Publishing.

Shenker, J. C., & Colletta, A. J. (1990). Asset securitization: Evolution, current issues and new frontiers. *Texas Law Review, 69,* 1369.

Simone Byrd, L. (2009). Collaborative corporate social responsibility: A case study examination of the international public relations agency involvement in the United Nations Global Compact. *Corporate Communications: An International Journal, 14*(3), 303–319.

Skouloudis, A., Jones, N., Malesios, C., & Evangelinos, K. (2014). Trends and determinants of corporate non-financial disclosure in Greece. *Journal of Cleaner Production, 68,* 174–188.

Stagars, M. (2015). *Impact investment funds for frontier markets in Southeast Asia: Creating a platform for institutional capital, high-quality foreign direct investment, and proactive policy making.* New York: Springer.

Sullivan, R., & Gouldson, A. (2012). Does voluntary carbon reporting meet investors' needs? *Journal of Cleaner Production, 36,* 60–67.

Sully, R. (2012). ISO 26000: The business guide to the new standard on social responsibility. *Impact Assessment and Project Appraisal, 30*(3), 214–215.

Thompson, P., & Cowton, C. J. (2004). Bringing the environment into bank lending: Implications for environmental reporting. *The British Accounting Review, 36*(2), 197–218.

UNEP FI. (2016). *Guide to banking and sustainability*. Geneva.

UNEP FI & United Nations Environmental Programme Finance Initiative. (2007). *Green financial products and services. Current trends and future opportunities in North America* (A report of the North American Task Force (NATF) of the United Nations Environment Programme Finance Initiative August). Geneva.

United Nations Global Compact. (2017). *Sustainable development goals: From promise to practice*. Retrieved from http://www.unglobalcompact.org/docs/publications/UNA-UK%20SDGS%202017.pdf

Van der Laan, S. (2009). The role of theory in explaining motivation for corporate social disclosures: Voluntary disclosures vs 'solicited'disclosures. *Australasian Accounting Business & Finance Journal, 3*(4), 15A.

Vecchi, V., Casalini, F., Balbo, L., & Caselli, S. (2015). Impact investing: A new asset class or a societal refocus of venture capital? In S. Caselli, G. Corbetta, & V. Vecchi (Eds.), *Public private partnerships for infrastructure and business development* (pp. 275–293). New York: Palgrave Macmillan.

Vecchi, V., Balbo, L., Brusoni, M., & Caselli, S. (Eds.). (2017). *Principles and practice of impact investing: A catalytic revolution*. Abingdon/ New York: Routledge.

Weber, O. (2016). Impact investing. In O. M. Lehner (Ed.), *Routledge handbook of social and sustainable finance*. London: Routledge.

Weber, O., & Feltmate, B. (2016). *Sustainable banking: Managing the social and environmental impact of financial institutions*. Toronto: University of Toronto Press.

Wright, C., & Rwabizambuga, A. (2006). Institutional pressures, corporate reputation, and voluntary codes of conduct: An examination of the equator principles. *Business and Society Review, 111*(1), 89–117.

CHAPTER 5

Sustainability in Banks: Emerging Trends

Abstract This chapter explores and compares the sustainability and environmental disclosure practices of European banks through a multiple case study approach. Through this exploratory analysis, six banks placed on the Global 100 Sustainability Companies list have been scrutinized to identify similarities and differences among banks' sustainability practices that may be linked to country-specific factors. The contributions of the chapter are twofold: on the one hand, the study helps to elucidate the most relevant sustainability practices adopted by banks, and on the other hand, the study offers insights and guidance and encourages future research.

Keywords Disclosure • Multiple case studies • Sustainability practices

5.1   Introduction

What do banks mean when they talk about sustainability? What do they disclose and communicate regarding sustainability?

These two questions have received considerable attention in recent years. Sustainability disclosure is conceived as a form of communication that goes beyond the delivery of financial information. As stated by the Global Reporting Initiative (GRI): "*[S]ustainability reporting or disclosure is the practice of measuring, reporting, and being accountable to internal and external stakeholders for organizational performance towards the goal of sustainable development*" (GRI 2006, p. 3). Statistics from the GRI website show

© The Author(s) 2018   93
R. Carè, *Sustainable Banking*,
https://doi.org/10.1007/978-3-319-73389-0_5

that currently more than 1200 financial institutions worldwide engage in sustainability reporting. It is notable that the disclosure of sustainability information through annual reports and websites is becoming increasingly more common on a global scale.

As described in Chap. 4, academia offers a large body of literature on sustainability disclosure that includes (1) studies examining motives and drivers behind the initiation and/or sustainment of social and sustainability reporting (Buhr 2002; O'Dwyer 2002; Spence 2007; Bebbington et al. 2009) and (2) research exploring contextual and internal factors (including managerial and governance attitudes) that influence the nature and extent of social and environmental reporting (Adams and McNicholas 2007; Bebbington et al. 2009).

This chapter compares the sustainability and environmental disclosure practices of European banks from a practical point of view and via a multiple case study approach. Through an exploratory analysis, six banks placed on the Global 100 Sustainable Companies list are scrutinized to identify similarities and differences between banks' sustainability practices.

5.2   Methodological Notes

Previous works in the field of sustainability disclosure has been largely conducted using a content analysis approach (see among others Guthrie and Abeysekera 2006; Jose and Lee 2007; Hahn and Lülfs 2014; Islam et al. 2016).

Content analysis is a research technique that involves identifying replicable and valid inferences from texts to the contexts of their use (Krippendorff 2012) by systematically enumerating the contents of documents and texts based on specific categories and requirements (Belal et al. 2015).

Moreover, "content analysis" is often used as a general term to refer to a number of different strategies used to analyze texts (Vaismoradi et al. 2013) and is also defined as a systematic coding and categorizing approach used to explore large volumes of textual information to determine trends and patterns of words used, frequencies and relationships (Gbrich 2007; Bloor and Wood 2006).

However, a major problem associated with performing a content analysis of disclosed documents is related to the fact that the size and quality of banks' published documents can vary across countries and can be influenced by factors such as dimensions or specific regulations under which they operate (Carè 2017). For example, calculating the number of pages devoted to sustainability documents may be not always be simple to accomplish, as banks can disclose sustainability or CSR information through their annual reports by providing in the same documents on financial and nonfinancial information.

Moreover, the lack of standardization in bank disclosure is often related to the application of country-specific regulations (e.g., the Dutch Banking Code) or voluntary guidance (e.g., the GRI). In particular, with regard to the GRI, despite the fact that they officially aim to provide standardized guidance, they do not provide information or suggestions on how to disclose sustainability information. For this reason, this chapter attempts to understand information disclosed through reports on banks' sustainability disclosure practices and thus surpass the limits of content analysis—related essentially to the use of word count tools—by applying a multiple case study approach. The use of a multiple case study approach necessarily restricts the observations of the investigation, although this may not hinder our empirical analysis as we conduct an in-depth analysis of a limited number of observations (Seawright and Gerring 2008; Adelopo 2017).

In this sense, a qualitative case study allows researchers to study complex phenomena within given contexts (Baxter and Jack 2008, p. 544) and to identify unique means of developing theories via in-depth insights into empirical phenomena (Dubois and Gadde 2002, p. 555). Benefits of the use of case studies for exploring relatively new or little explored phenomena have been illustrated (Eisenhardt 1989; Yin 2009). The use of multiple case studies offers opportunities to (1) cope with a technically distinctive situation in which there are many more variables of interest than data points and (2) benefit from the prior development of theoretical propositions to guide data collection and analysis (Yin 2013). Eisenhardt (1989) highlights the potential of case studies to capture dynamics of a studied phenomenon and suggests that "analyzing data is the heart of building theory from case studies, but it is both the most difficult and the least codified part of the process" (p. 539). To ensure the reliability of this approach, a research protocol has been developed (Yin 2013).

5.2.1   Sampling Procedures

The sample was generated from banks placed on the Top Sustainable 100 Companies list (see Appendix 5.1) for 2017 (Table 5.1).

The final sample of analysis includes the first six banks located in Europe and listed in the Global 100 Sustainable Companies Ranking. Specifically,

Table 5.1   Banks enclosed in the Top Sustainable 100 Companies list

Ranking 2017	Ranking 2016	Ranking 2015	Bank	Country	Score 2017	Score 2016	Score 2015
4	7	10	Danske Bank A/S	DK	71.05	72.40	68.40
5	45	n.r.	ING Group	NL	70.93	63.50	–
6	4	21	Commonwealth Bank of Australia	AUS	70	73.90	65.80
17	n.r.	42	Crédit Agricole SA	FR	65.31	–	61.70
20	n.r.	n.r.	Intesa Sanpaolo	IT	64.13	–	–
34	28	46	DNB ASA	N	61.69	66.10	61.40
37	n.r.	n.r.	Royal Bank of Canada	CDN	60.87	–	–
40	18	70	Shinhan Financial Group Co Ltd	ROK	60.68	68.80	56.40
42	35	82	BNP Paribas SA	FR	60.25	64.30	54.10
46	41	58	Skandinaviska Enskilda Banken	S	59.35	63.80	58.70
50	73	79	National Australia Bank Ltd	AUS	58.66	58.90	54.50
55	n.r.	91	Hang Seng Bank Ltd	HK	58.10	–	52.80
58	54	76	Toronto-Dominion Bank	CDN	57.97	62.20	55.90
60	n.r.	n.r.	Banco Santander Brasil SA	BR	57.77	–	–
61	86	86	Bank of Montreal	CDN	57.72	56.80	53.70

Legenda: AUS=Australia; BR=Brazil; CDN=Canada; DK= Denmark; FR=France; HK=Hong Kong; IT=Italy; N=Norway; NL=Netherlands; ROK=Republic of Korea; S=Sweden
Source: Our elaboration from Global 100 Sustainable Companies Ranking

the following banks are considered: BNP Paribas (FR), Crédit Agricole (FR), ING (NL), Danske Bank (DK), DNB ASA (N), and Skandinaviska Enskilda Banken (S). Intesa SanPaolo is excluded from the analysis because it is analyzed as a single case study in Chap. 6 and is thus replaced with Skandinaviska Enskilda Banken.

This sample—which can be considered a convenience sample—is intended to maximize efficiency and validity (Yin 2013) both internally and externally. In particular, external validity (or generalization) represents a major barrier to case study research. In this sense, Yin (2013) refers to the term "analytical generalization" to describe the process by which the findings of a case study can be generalized to develop a theory. Each case is selected to explore sustainable business and disclosure practices for the same geographical area (Europe) based on an assumption that banks included in the sample operate within the same (European) legal framework. Data on the European banks analyzed are presented in Table 5.2.

Table 5.2   Banks data (in euros)

		2016	2015	2014
Danske Bank	Total number of employees	19.000	19.049	13.603
	Dividends paid	1.189.666	1.084.312	745.405,90
	Total assets	468.135.575	442.496.946	464.016.156
	Net income	2.668.518	1.763.469	530.532
ING Bank	Total number of employees	51.943	52.720	55.945
	Dividends paid	1.345.000	2.200.000	1.225.000
	Total assets	843.919.000	1.001.992.000	828.602.000
	Net income	4.302.000	4.731.000	2.823.000
Credit Agricole	Total number of employees	73.605	71.495	75.396
	Dividends paid	1.878.429	n.a.	n.a.
	Total assets	1.524.232.000	1.529.294.000	1.589.044.000
	Net income	3.955.000	3.971.000	2.760.000
DNB ASA	Total number of employees	11 459	11 840	12 064
	Dividends paid	n.a.	n.a.	n.a.
	Total assets	2,653,201	2,598,530	2,649,341
	Net income	n.a.	n.a.	n.a.
BNP Paribas	Total number of employees	192.419	189.077	187.903
	Dividends paid	0	0	0
	Total assets	2.076.959.000	1.994.193.000	2.077.758.000
	Net income	8.115.000	7.044.000	507.000
Skandinaviska Enskilda Banken	Total number of employees	15.300	15.500	16.000
	Dividends paid	n.a.	n.a.	n.a.
	Total assets	267.814.938	255.058.082	269.865.046
	Net income	1.085.081	1.693.928	1.963.326

Source: Our elaboration from Orbis data

5.2.2   *Data Analysis and Coding Procedure*

Using the research protocol, banks' websites and reports for 2014 to 2016 were analyzed. Then, sustainability reports were classified and preliminarily assessed. From this preliminary assessment, five main dimensions of analysis were detected:

1. Code of conduct, internal policy, and position statements
2. Corporate governance

3. Supported international standards, initiatives, and frameworks
4. Risks management procedures
5. Products and services

The first dimension relates to the general approach that banks apply in terms of corporate social responsibility (CSR) and sustainability. The second dimension refers to the possibility that banks maintain specific boards and committees dedicated to sustainability issues and remuneration policies related to sustainable performance. The third dimension is based on the analysis of the main international initiatives banks tend to support. The fourth dimension is related to the possibility that banks develop specific risk management frameworks to manage emerging environmental and social risks (ESR). Finally, the fifth dimension is devoted to analyzing emerging products and services that banks offer to their clients and how these are integrated within banks' investment strategies and portfolios. The coding schemes applied were developed through an iterative process designed to identify sustainability measures of the banks' business models. In a second phase, descriptions were developed to identify similarities and differences between the cases, facilitating the generation of theoretical concepts (Eisenhardt 1989).

5.3   Case Histories

The following sections describe each bank analyzed based on the five dimensions highlighted in Sect. 5.2. Each case study is described moving from available information, and thus each differs based on the quality and quantity of information disclosed in each of the five selected dimensions.

5.3.1   Case of Danske Bank A/S (Denmark)

Danske Bank was founded in 1871 and is headquartered in Copenhagen (Denmark). It is the largest bank in the Danish retail banking sector (Martensen and Grønholdt 2010) and includes Danske Bank, Realkredit Danmark, and other subsidiaries. The group delivers financial services including banking, insurance, mortgage, asset management, brokerage, credit card, real estate, and leasing services and serves private customers as well as the corporate and institutional sectors worldwide. The five core values of Danske Bank are expertise, integrity, value creation, commitment, and accessibility. Its new Corporate Responsibility Strategy developed in 2015 is based on two strategic themes (fostering financial confidence and accessible finance for everyone) and five areas of focus (contributing to society, responsible customer relationships, responsible employers, the environmental footprint, and responsible supplier relationships) with the aim to integrate responsibility in the core business (Danske Bank Corporate Responsibility Report 2016). The company's corporate responsibility department directs the implementation of its Corporate Responsibility Strategy. The department also prepares progress reports and implements select initiatives (Danske Bank Corporate Responsibility Report 2015).

Code of Conduct, Internal Policy, and Position Statements

Danske Bank upgraded its code of conduct in 2017. The code aims to protect the reputation of the group and to ensure its compliance with applicable laws and regulations by communicating the most essential standards for prudent behavior and conduct expected from its employees in their daily activities (Danske Bank Code of Conduct 2017). Danske Bank has adopted a series of policy (Table 5.3) and position statements (e.g., CO_2 emissions, modern slavery, forestry, agriculture, mining and metals, fossil fuels, and arms and defense).

Corporate Governance

The Danske Bank Business Integrity Board includes Executive Board members and heads of the group's business units and support functions. It makes corporate responsibility recommendations to the Executive Board on strategic plans and policies and oversees the implementation of corporate responsibility decisions. Its major functions include: (1) the coordination of the Corporate Responsibility Strategy's implementation and business integration throughout the business; (2) the preparation of progress reports; and (3) the implementation of select corporate responsibility initiatives (Danske Bank CR Factbook 2016).

Supported International Standards, Initiatives, and Frameworks

In 1992, Danske Bank signed the environmental charter for banks under the United Nations (UN) Environmental Programme. Through its Corporate Responsibility Strategy 2015–2018, Danske Bank supports the UN's 2030 Agenda for Sustainable Development and contributes to a

Table 5.3 Policies adopted by Danske Bank

Policy	Year of adoption	Description
AML, CTF and Sanctions Policy	2017	This policy sets out principles and standards for the compliance and management of risks associated with financial crime for Danske Bank Group (Danske Bank AML CTF and Sanctions Policy 2017)
Compliance Policy	2017	This policy sets out the principles and standards for compliance and management of compliance risks in Danske Bank Group (Danske Bank Group Compliance Policy 2017)
Remuneration Policy	2017	This policy applies to all group employees. The policy and the group's general incentive structures reflect the group's objectives for good corporate governance and sustained and long-term value creation for shareholders (Danske Bank Remuneration Policy 2017)
Stakeholder Policy	2016	This policy outlines the group's general principles and guidelines for its relations with stakeholders (Danske Bank Stakeholder Policy 2017)
Diversity and Inclusion Policy	2016	The policy sets out elements of diversity and inclusion, reflecting Danske Bank group's overall aims and specifying focus areas (Danske Bank Diversity and Inclusion Policy 2016)
Responsible Investment Policy	2016	This policy governs the bank's responsible investment practices (Danske Bank Responsible Investment Policy 2017)
Whistleblowing Policy	2017	This policy sets out a scheme that supports the reporting of wrongdoings to management for its attention or intervention. Under this policy, employees are encouraged to raise concerns regarding irregularities and criminal offenses related to fraud, sexual harassment, and other failures to comply with applicable regulations, laws, or internal standards (below referred to as "wrongdoings") to which the group's employees might become aware (Danske Bank Whistleblowing Policy 2017)

Tax Policy	2017	This policy sets out a responsible and transparent approach to taxation and applies to all employees, functions, units of the group, and all separate legal entities once adopted by executive management teams and/or boards of directors (Danske Bank Tax Policy 2017)
External Publication of Information Management Policy	2016	This policy defines information that instructs and guides employees to perform their jobs as competently and efficiently as possible to meet the group's objectives. The policy also establishes common terminology and general principles for working with information across the group (Danske Bank Publication of Information Management Policy 2016)
Investor Relations Policy	2016	This policy informs equity and debt investors, analysts and other IR stakeholders of the group's activities in compliance with all national and international statutory requirements and relevant stock exchange regulations on the basis of corporate governance standards and recommendations from relevant organizations (Danske Bank Investors Relations Policy 2016)
Responsibility Policy	2016	This policy outlines Danske Bank Group's approach to and principles for conducting business in a responsible and transparent manner (Danske Bank Responsibility Policy 2016)
Conflict of Interest Policy	2014	This policy provides examples of conflicts of interest that may arise within the group and specifies minimum standards for actions to be taken to manage such conflicts (Danske Bank Conflict of Interest Policy 2014)

Source: Our elaboration from Danske Bank disclosed documents

variety sustainable development goals (SDGs) adopted by the UN in 2015 (e.g., health and well-being, gender equality, climate action, and partnerships). Moreover, Danske Bank supports

1. The UN Global Compact
2. The OECD Guideline for Multinational Enterprises[1]
3. The UN Guiding Principles on Business and Human Rights
4. The UN-supported Principles for Responsible Investment
5. The UN Environment Program Finance Initiatives
6. The ILO Declaration on Fundamental Principles and Rights at Work
7. The Universal Declaration of Human Rights

Risk Management Procedures

Danske Bank has incorporated environmental considerations into its credit procedures to ensure that it takes account national and international requirements regarding the impacts of companies on the environment. In 2016, Danske Bank developed five sector-specific position statements that clarify how screening and environmental, social, and governance (ESG) risk analysis are performed. In particular, they establish a general framework for proactive dialogue about risks and opportunities with customers, business partners, and portfolio companies in which the bank invests. The statements focus on issues related to fossil fuels, forestry, climate change, arms and defense, and mining and metals and cover all operations (Danske Bank CR Report 2016).

Products and Services

From December 2014, the Danske Bank Treasury, which is responsible for the bank's bond holdings, has invested DKK 1 billion in green bonds issued to fund projects that have a positive environmental impact (Danske Bank CR Report 2015, 2016). In 2016, Danske Bank launched the European Corporate Sustainable Bond Fund, which enables customers to invest in companies that support sustainable development. In particular, the European Corporate Sustainable Bond fund invests in bonds issued by companies that meet enhanced responsible investment criteria. The fund employs a cautious approach to controversial industries, exhibits heightened ESG awareness, and integrates innovative sustainability thinking and research through its investment decisions (Danske Bank CR

Report 2016). Danske Bank is the first Nordic bank to join the Climate Bonds Partnership Program[2] and has helped (as advisor) Vasakronan issue a SEK 1 billion green bond in addition to assisting the City of Gothenburg with its first green loan. In addition, Danske Bank assisted Nordic Investment Bank with the issuing of its first 500 million euro-denominated environmental bond (Danske Bank Interim Report—first half 2017, 2017).

Moreover, the group provides a list of screened companies that have been excluded from the bank's investment universe because they are considered incompliant with its Responsibility Policy (e.g., involved in breaching environmental norms, violations of labor rights norms, or the production of nuclear weapons).

5.3.2   Case of ING Group (the Netherlands)

ING was founded in 1991 and is headquartered in Amsterdam, the Netherlands. Currently, the group delivers retail and wholesale banking services to private clients, small businesses, large corporations, financial institutions, and governments. In 2016, Sustainalytics—a global provider of ESG research and ratings—named ING the best performing bank from a list of 395 (ING Application of the Dutch Banking Code 2016).

Code of Conduct, Internal Policy, and Position Statements
The bank's ESR framework outlines environmental and social standards and parameters under which ING conducts business in the animal husbandry, chemicals, defense, energy, forestry and agrocommodities, manufacturing, and mining and metals sectors. The bank's ESR Sector Policy also outlines potential impacts associated with these sectors. ING's ESR Sector Policy describes processes that assist the bank in addressing such risks in a responsible and consistent manner. These consider the following:

- Exclusion/no-go areas of engagement
- The identification of risk and best industry guidance per sector
- ESR due diligence processes, including client and transaction assessment methods
- ESR governance (ING Annual Report 2016, 2017)

Corporate Governance

ING Bank voluntary supports principles of the Dutch Banking Code regarding remuneration to the members of its executive board and it uses these principles as a reference for its own corporate governance. The ESR Sector Policy highlights that responsibility for gathering information and assessing clients and transactions lies with the first line of defense, that is, the front office, deal principals, and other front office representatives. Credit risk management acts as the second line of defense and ensures that the client ESR assessment method has been honored, approves of transaction ESR assessments and ultimately opines on potential required mitigating actions as part of the ESR's outcome approval process. The Sustainability Department advises ING management on the bank's sustainability strategy. As such, it analyses sustainability trends in relation to ING's business conduct (ING Annual Report 2015, 2016).

Supported International Standards, Initiatives, and Frameworks

ING is an equator principle financial institution (EPFI)[3] that implements the EP through its own internal environmental and social policies, procedures, and standards, and it does not offer project finance or project-related corporate loans to clients who do not comply with these principles (ING Group Sustainability Annex 2014). Moreover, the EPs are embedded in ING's ESR framework and credit approval process (ING Annual Report 2016). A dedicated team is responsible for embedding the principles within ING's operations.

In October 2016, ING was ranked among the top 9% of thousands of companies on actions and strategies that combat climate change according to leading nonprofit organization Carbon Disclosure Project (CDP). ING was again named under CDP's "Climate A-list" of 193 companies leading on climate change action, receiving the highest possible score, and it has been recognized with a Euronext/CDP Leadership Award for maintaining outstanding environmental disclosure practices.

In June 2016, ING joined the Ellen MacArthur Foundation as an official Circular Economy 100 (CE100) corporate member to improve its commitment to stimulating the circular economy (ING Application of the Dutch Banking Code 2016).

Currently, ING is committed to the following:

- The Equator Principles Association
- The OECD Guidelines
- The IUCN Red List for Species

- IUCN Protected Areas Categories 1 and 2
- The CDP (formerly known as the Carbon Disclosure Project)
- The GRI
- RE100 commitment to 100% renewable electricity procurement
- A Global CEO letter to world leaders urging concrete climate action (2015)
- The European Financial Services Round Table (EFR) Statement on Climate Change
- The Ellen MacArthur Foundation CE100 (ING Environmental Approach 2017).

ING is also a signatory of the following

- The UN Environmental Program Finance Initiative (UNEP FI) and the UNEP Finance Initiative Climate Change Working Group (UNEP FI CCWG)
- The Energy Efficiency Financial Institutions Group (UNEP FI / European Commission)
- The UN Global Compact
- The IUCN Leaders for Nature network (ING Environmental Approach 2017).

Risk Management Procedures

ING adopts an ESR framework that is integrated into its overall risk management methodology (ING Group Annual Report 2014). The ESR framework, which is reviewed every three years on the basis of significant changes identified in sectors that are more vulnerable to ESR and impacts, is applied to ING's wholesale banking business department (ING Group Annual Report 2016). The ESR framework covers the sectors of mining and metals, chemicals, defense, energy, forestry and agrocommodities, and manufacturing. It also cites explicit restrictions on activities that are not in line with ING's values (ING Group Annual Report 2015, p. 52). ING's ESR Framework is based on the screening of clients and transactions. In 2015, more than 3326 corporate clients and 4713 corporate lending transactions were assessed under the ESR framework (ING Group Annual Report 2015, p. 53). Moreover, ESRs for all lending transactions are reviewed on a yearly basis following annual credit reviews (ING Group Annual Report 2016). In addition to ESR assessment, lending clients and transactions are reviewed against externally recognized sustainability criteria (ING Group Annual Report 2015).

Products and Services

In 2015, ING issued its first green bond by raising US$800 million and €500 million for an initial issue, and US$62.5 million in a private placement is being used to finance and refinance loans in six different areas: renewable energy, green buildings, public transport, waste management, water management, and energy efficiency (ING Green Bond Programme 2016; ING Environmental Approach 2017). ING also acted as joint bookrunner and arranger on a €1 billion dual-tranche green bond issued by TenneT, a European electricity transmission system operator (ING Annual Report 2015 2016). In 2016, ING won Environmental Finance Green Bond Awards as the "Biggest Issuer" and for "Bond of the Year" (ING Group Annual Report 2016, 2017). Through its subsidiary, ING Groenbank, ING finances sustainable investment by offering lending services to a variety of Dutch sectors at favorable rates. Such sectors involve organic farming, renewable energy generation, sustainable construction, and the reuse of waste materials (ING Annual Report 2016, 2017). ING Groenbank also directs up to 10% of its balance sheet toward financial inclusion activities with microfinance—focused on female entrepreneurs— representing a main component (ING Annual Report 2015, 2016).

In 2016, there was a strategic shift from traditional microfinance portfolios in India and Turkey to the use of a more diversified portfolio in terms of locations and the combination of financial services offered. Microfinance was rebranded as Impact Finance, which now acts as a catalytic fund for initiating impact investments both inside and outside of ING (ING Annual Report 2016, 2017).

5.3.3   Case of Crédit Agricole SA (France)

Crédit Agricole (CA) is headquartered in Montrouge, France. The group delivers retail, corporate, insurance, and investment banking products and services worldwide. The company operates through five segments (asset gathering; French retail banking—LCL; international retail banking; specialized financial services; and large customers). It also delivers payment instruments, loans, saving products, and payment management products and services as well as savings/retirement, death and disability/creditor/group, and property and casualty insurance products.

At CA, negative environmental and/or social impacts related to financing and investments are taken into account based on three pillars: the application of the EPs, CSR sector policies, and the assessment of environmental and social aspects of operations (CA 2015 Registration Document 2016, p. 54). The CA CSR strategy is based on three ambitions and ten focus areas, is based on consultations with employees and outside stakeholders, and is embodied in a process of participatory and evolutionary progress referred to as FReD.

FReD is based on the three sets of standards (i.e., the three CSR pillars: economic, social, and environmental) to create a framework for its entities' actions: Fides (for the economic segment), Respect (for the social segment), and Demeter (for the environmental segment). Each of these areas is associated with 19 commitments. Entities must focus on five areas for each set of standards and must organize at least 15 projects.

Code of Conduct, Internal Policy, and Position Statements
In 2017, the group developed a Group-wide Ethics Charter. This charter, signed by the group's top management personnel, stresses CA's core values of acting responsibly, locally, and with solidarity. It restates principles for actions and behaviors to be observed on a day-to-day basis with customers, employees, suppliers, society at large, and all stakeholders (CA Code of Ethics 2017). From 2013, CA CIB has introduced sector policies to go further in recognizing the social and environmental impacts of its activities, and these are applied group wide. Sector policies set conditions for investment and define criteria for the analysis and screening of all transactions involving the following sectors: armaments (2010); energy (oil and gas, shale gas, and coal-fired power stations); hydro plants and nuclear (2012); mining and metals (2013); transport (aviation, maritime, and automotive) (2013); transport infrastructure (2014); real estate (2015); and forests and palm oil (2015) (CA 2014 Registration Document 2015).

Corporate Governance
The Strategic and CSR Committee of the CA Board of Directors ensures that CSR issues are considered in the group's strategies and operations. The Executive Committee approves of CSR policies and ensures that it has the resources required to implement them. The Sustainable Development Division reporting to the Secretary General of CA supports all those involved and hosts the CSR officer and liaison network (Crédit Agricole 2015–2016 Corporate Social Responsibility 2016). Moreover, part (one-third) of the long-term variable compensation of executive officers is impacted by the CSR performance of CA and is based on the FReD Index group. This portion of variable compensation is paid when the group's index is equal to 2.

Supported International Standards, Initiatives, and Frameworks
CA has been a signatory of the UN Global Compact since 2003; the EPs since 2003; the Principles for Responsible Investment (PRI) since 2006; the Diversity Charter since 2008; the Sustainable Purchasing Charter since 2010; the Charter for the Energy Efficiency of Commercial Buildings since 2013; the Science-Based Targets since 2016; and the RE100 since 2016. Moreover, CA has been cofounding member of the Green Bonds Principles since 2014; the Portfolio Decarbonization Coalition since 2014; the Mainstreaming of Climate Action Within Financial Institutions since 2015; the Catalytic Finance Initiative since 2015; the French Business Climate Pledge since 2015; and the BBCA Association (low-carbon building design) since 2015.

Risk Management Procedures
In 2013, CA Corporate and Investment Banking (CIB) introduced a scoring system for all corporate customers. Customers are scored each year on a scale of three levels (advanced, adequate, and sensitive) based on whether a customer complies with existing sector policies (adequate), whether image risks threaten the bank (sensitive), and whether a customer is listed in the main global CSR indices (advanced).

In addition, from 2014 the EP framework has been applied to project finance advisory services, project finances, project-related corporate loans, and bridge loans. In addition to cases determined under the EP Charter, CA endeavors to apply these principles to all other financing that is directly related to a project on a voluntary basis (CA 2015 Registration Document 2016).

Products and Services
CA arranged over $21 billion in green, social, and sustainability bonds for its major customers in 2016 (CA 2016 Registration Document 2017) as well as a number of transactions on its own account (green notes of €1313 billion) (CA 2015 Registration Document 2016). In 2013, CA launched the *Crédit Agricole CIB Green Notes*. Green Notes are bonds or any other type of financing raised by CA whose proceeds are dedicated to funding environmental projects and companies. CA is developing a complete line of high-impact investment solutions dubbed "Alternative Investments". Such products fund actions for employment, housing, health, the environment, associations, debt relief, and international solidarity (CA 2015–2016 Corporate Social Responsibility 2016).

By 31 December 2016, CA CIB had financed €1.541 billion in green loans thanks to green notes and similar debt products (CA Green Notes Framework 2016). Moreover, in 2015, Amundi—the largest asset manager by assets under management—launched the *Amundi Green Bonds* fund, which enables institutional investors to participate in the financing of the energy and environmental transition by investing in the green bonds market and in debt securities of specialist and leading companies focusing on green technology development (CA 2015 Registration Document 2016; CA 2016 Registration Document 2017). The fund's objective is to outperform the Barclays Global Green Bond Index over the recommended investment period, and it can invest up to 100% in diverse types of bonds issued by governments, supranationals, or corporations and at least 66% in "Green Bonds". Amundi also offers the Amundi Valeurs Durables fund, which invests in European companies that earmark at least 20% of their revenues for the development of green technologies. By the end of 2016, the fund's assets totaled €237 million. In 2016, Amundi also launched an Impact Green Bond fund, which enriches the existing offer in terms of financing the energy and ecological transition (Amundi ESG Integration Governance, Policy & Strategy, 2016). CA CIB has also taken part in the largest issue made by a French corporation (Danone) and in the issuance of the largest euro-denominated green bonds tranche with EDF (Électricité de France) Group (CA 2016 Registration Document 2017).

5.3.4   Case of DNB ASA (Norway)

DNB ASA was founded in 1882 and is headquartered in Oslo, Norway. DNB is Norway's largest financial services group and is one of the largest in the Nordic region in terms of market capitalisation. The group offers a full range of financial services, including loans, savings, advisory services, insurance, and pension products for retail and corporate customers, and it operates through several subsidiaries based in Norway and abroad. It operates through five segments: personal customers, small and medium-sized enterprises, large corporation and international customers, trade, and traditional pension products. It offers its products and services to various sectors (i.e., energy; financial institutions; healthcare; manufacturing; packaging and forest products; seafood; shipping, offshore activities, and logistics; and telecom, media, and technology).

Code of Conduct, Internal Policy, and Position Statements

To date, DNB has published a series of internal steering documents. In particular, the group's guidelines for CSR aim to

- ensure that DNB does not contribute to human and labor rights violations, corruption, serious environmental harm, or other actions which may be perceived as unethical;
- provide a framework for DNB's corporate banking units when assessing CSR performance and climate and ESG risks with customers;
- present DNB's exclusion policy;
- present and explain how industry-specific ESG risks are addressed;
- present and explain DNB's view on controversial activities and customers/activities where credit decisions must be elevated and where an enhanced CSR/ESG assessment must be applied;
- document DNB's CSR/ESG risk assessment process (DNB Group Guidelines for Corporate Social Responsibility 2016).

Supported International Standards, Initiatives, and Frameworks

In addition to the Norwegian standards, DNB supports and participates in a number of global initiatives and international guidelines to ensure responsible operations (DNB 2016 Annual Report 2017). In 2016, DNB joined the UN SDGs.[4] Other supported initiatives include the following:

1. The UNEP FI
2. The OECD's guidelines for multinational companies
3. The UN Guiding Principles on Business and Human Rights
4. The PRI
5. The GRI
6. The EPs
7. The CDP and A-list[5]
8. The Dow Jones Sustainability Index (DJSI)
9. The Norwegian forum for responsible and sustainable investments (Norsif)

Risk Management Procedures

DNB applies a dedicated CSR/ESG risk assessment tool. The CSR/ESG risk assessment tools assist with the assessment of a customer's CSR/ESG risk level and CSR/ESG risk mitigation capacity based on the following five core CSR/ESG themes: the environment, climate change, human and labor rights, corruption, and governance and transparency (DNB CSR/ ESG risk assessment tool 2016).

Products and Services
DNB finances wind, water, and solar power projects and its portfolio totaled more than NOK 46 billion in 2016. Moreover, internationally DNB finances renewable projects managed in Europe, the United States, South America, and Australia (DNB 2016 Annual Report 2017). On February 2015, DNB Bank ASA issued a NOK 1 billion green bond based on financing 14 wind projects (DNB Report on Green Bond Proceeds 2017). Moreover, in following its own Responsible Investment policy, DNB excluded 129 companies deemed in breach of the group's guidelines (DNB 2016 Annual Report Responsible Investment 2017).

5.3.5   Case of BNP Paribas SA (France)

BNP Paribas SA was founded in 1848 and is based in Paris, France. The company was formerly known as Banque Nationale de Paris and changed its name to BNP Paribas SA in May 2000. BNP Paribas delivers a range of banking and financial services in France and internationally and operates through three divisions: domestic markets, international financial services, and CIB. The bank also delivers asset management and investment advisory services to institutions and individuals based in Europe, the United States, Asia, and emerging markets.

Code of Conduct, Internal Policy, and Position Statements
The bank's code of conduct highlights a set of rules of conduct based on the following themes: (1) customers' interests, (2) financial security, (3) market integrity, (4) professional ethics, (5) respect for colleagues, (6) group protection, and (7) involvement with society. The BNP Paribas responsibility policy is structured on 4 pillars and 12 commitments that reflect the bank's social and environmental responsibility (CSR) priorities and specific achievements. The fight against climate change is one of the four pillars of BNP Paribas' CSR disclosure policy.

Corporate Governance
The CSR Committee is tasked with monitoring corporate governance issues.

Its role is to help the Board of Directors adapt corporate governance practices, to report to the Executive Committee, and to coordinate the implementation and monitoring of all CSR actions.

Supported International Standards, Initiatives, and Frameworks
The environmental commitments of BNP Paribas are guided by several principles and global initiatives (e.g., the PRI, the EPs, the Soft Commodities Compact of the BEI, and the Montreal Carbon Pledge). The group endorsed the EPs in 2008 and includes an extra-financial analysis in its project financing documents (Registration Document 2011, p. 370).

The group acknowledges and is committed to respecting a number of principles and norms that underpin the way it does business:

- The UN SDGs
- The ten principles of the UN Global Compact
- The internationally accepted OECD Guidelines for multinational enterprises
- The internationally accepted Standards of Human Rights as defined in the International Bill of Human Rights
- Core labor standards set out by the International Labor Organization (ILO; BNP Paribas Code of Conduct 2016)

Moreover, BNP Paribas is compliant with the reporting requirements of Article 173, the Energy Transition for Green Growth Act, and the recommendations of the Task Force on Climate-related Financial Disclosures (TCFD). BNP also complies with new regulations regarding transparency on and respect for human rights (The UK "Modern Slavery Act"), and in 2017, it published its "Modern Slavery and Human Trafficking Statement". Moreover, BNP Paribas complies with the French corporate duty of vigilance law that requires multinational French companies to "establish and implement a diligence plan which should state the measures taken to identify and prevent the occurrence of human rights and environmental risks resulting from their activities, the activities of companies they control and the activities of sub-contractors and supplier, in France and abroad" (BNP CSR 2016 & 2017 Highlights 2017). BNP Paribas participates in the following key industry initiatives:

- The UN Global Compact (2003)
- The PRI—BNP Paribas Asset Management (2006), BNP Real Estate Investment Management (2015), BNP Paribas Securities Services, and BNP Paribas Cardif (2016)

- The EPs (2008)
- Institutional Investors on Climate Change—IIGCC (2007)
- The UN Women's Empowerment Principles (2011)
- The Roundtable on Sustainable Palm Oil (2011)
- The Green Bond Principles—voluntary guidelines for developing the green bond market (2014)
- The Global Impact Investing Network (2014)
- The Soft Commodities Compact (2014) of the Banking Environment Initiative[6]
- The ILO Business Charter on Disability (2016)
- The Carbon Pricing Leadership Coalition[7] (2017)

Risk Management Procedures
In 2010, BNP Paribas developed a framework for managing ESG risks as part of a global risk management approach based on

- respect for the EPs for major industrial and infrastructure projects;
- the development of financing and investment policies for managing the group's activities in sectors presenting significant ESG issues;
- the use of management and monitoring tools to address such risks;
- the implementation of a specific ESG risk assessment framework for its products and services (Registration Document 2015, p. 458).

This framework was further reinforced in 2015. CSR screening is further used to evaluate the most relevant nonfinancial risks facing sectors that are not covered by specific sector policies. The CIB division has created a CSR screening tool for identifying the main ESG risks applicable to large corporate clients operating in sectors not covered by the sector policies, and clients are subjected to specific due diligence (Registration Document 2014, p. 435). This screening is realized through the use of a questionnaire in the following sectors: consumer goods, capital assets, energy and electricity, oil, gas/chemical products, ICT, health care, transportation, automotive, building and building materials, and metallurgy (Registration Document 2015, p. 460).

Provisions and guarantees covering environmental risks—both for 2014 and for 2013—amount to US$2.6 million, are related to private litigation, and do not cover penalties for noncompliance with regulations (Registration Document 2014, p. 467; Registration Document 2013, p. 430). In 2012 and 2011, provisions and guarantees covering environmental risks amount to US$3.4 million.

Products and Services

BNP Paribas allocated €9.3 million in funding to the renewable energy sector in 2016. In 2015, the group was lead manager of €3.875 billion in green bonds, of which €827 million represented index-linked bonds (BNP Paribas Corporate Social Responsibility 2015). BNP Paribas issued its first green bonds in November 2016 for a total of €500 million. The total amount of green bonds issued in 2016 for which the group was joint lead manager amounted to €2.4 billion. Some of the many transactions in which the group was involved in 2016 include the following:

- The first Turkish green bond issued by Turkiye Sinai Kalkinma Bankasi (US$300 million with BNP Paribas as joint lead manager), whose net income is intended to support investments reducing greenhouse gas emissions in the private sector
- The first euro-denominated green bonds issued by a US electricity generation company (US$1.1 billion, Southern Power)
- The first sovereign green bond in France (€7 billion planned with 22-year maturity) to be used to finance climate, biodiversity, and pollution programs (BNP Paribas Registration Document 2016, 2017)

As an integral part of its governance of green bonds and to support the development of green bond initiatives, BNP Paribas has established a Green Bond Committee (BNP Paribas Green Bond Framework 2016).

The Green Bond Committee is chaired by the head of CSR for BNP Paribas, and its role is

- To review and validate the pool of Eligible Green Assets;
- To validate annual reporting for investors;
- To review appropriate external independent auditor reports and to address any issues that arise;
- To monitor any ongoing evolution related to the green bond market practices in terms of disclosure/reporting and harmonization (BNP Paribas Green Bond Framework 2016).

Annual reporting covers (1) eligible green assets and their relevant environmental impact indicators, (2) the allocation of note net proceeds to eligible green assets detailing the aggregate amount dedicated to each eligible sector, and (3) the balance of unallocated cash and/or cash equivalents and/or other liquid marketable instruments (BNP Paribas Fixed Income Presentation 2017).

In addition, in 2016 BNP Paribas commissioned Oekom research to assist with the issuance of its debut Green Bond. The Oekom assessment is based on five key challenges facing companies in terms of sustainability management: (1) sustainability standards for the lending business, (2) customer and product responsibility, (3) sustainable investment criteria, (4) employee relations and work environments, and (5) business ethics. With regard to BNP Paribas, significant outperformance was achieved on "Sustainable investment criteria", whereas in "Business ethics", the company lags behind the industry's average level (Verification of the Sustainability Quality of the Green Bond issued by BNP Paribas SA 2016).

Moreover, the 16.6% of all loans granted to companies by BNP Paribas in 2016 contributed directly to the achievement of one of the UN SDGs. This involves financing projects related to associations, social work, education, and health care. Moreover, BNP Paribas has supported 407 start-ups having a significant positive impact on the French Retail Banking portfolio (CSR Department Report 2017). Since 2013, BNP Paribas has launched 12 ethical indices that have raised more than €3 billion. These solutions provide investors with a financial return while allowing them to have a positive impact and particularly on the environment (BNP Paribas Registration Document 2016, 2017). Finally, BNP Paribas collaborated with the General Directorate of the Treasury for the development of the first French Social Impact Bond (SIB).

5.3.6   Case of Skandinaviska Enskilda Banken (Sweden)

Skandinaviska Enskilda Banken AB (publ) was founded in 1856 and is headquartered in Stockholm, Sweden. The bank delivers corporate, institutional, and private banking services, including savings account, investment banking, securities brokerage, loan, pension, and insurance products. SEB has branches throughout Sweden, in Germany, and in the Baltic States, and it is represented in many countries worldwide.

Code of Conduct, Internal Policy, and Position Statements
SEB's Code of Conduct describes and lays out SEB's values, ethics, and standards of business conduct (SEB Corporate Governance Report 2016). SEB is also governed by a set of policies and instructions including a corporate sustainability policy, environmental policy, and human rights policy among others (SEB Code of Conduct 2016), while position

statements refer to child labor, climate change, fresh water, arms and defense, forestry, fossil fuels, mining and metals, renewable energy, and shipping.

Corporate Governance
The external framework for SEB's corporate governance considers the following rules and guidelines:

- The Companies Act
- The Annual Accounts Act
- The Nasdaq Stockholm Issuer Rules
- The Swedish Corporate Governance Code
- The Banking and Financing Business Act
- Rules and guidelines issued by the Swedish Financial Supervisory Authority and by other authorities (SEB Corporate Governance Report 2016)

Policies and instructions that have been drawn up to define the division of responsibility within the group serve as important tools for the board and the president and chief executive officer (the president) in their governing and controlling roles. Such policies and instructions include the following, among others:

- Rules of procedure for the board and instructions for board committees
- Instructions for the president and the group's activities
- the group's credit instruction and risk policy
- Instructions for handling of conflicts of interest
- Instructions for procedures against money laundering and the financing of terrorism
- The code of conduct
- The remuneration policy
- The corporate sustainability policy
- Policies on the assessment of suitability of directors, members of the Group Executive Committee (GEC), and other key function holders

The Corporate Sustainability Committee is chaired by the head of Group Communications.

Supported International Standards, Initiatives, and Frameworks
Within the framework of the UNEP, SEB has joined nine other banks around the world in issuing a Positive Impact Manifesto. SEB is also committed to the following:

1. The UN Global Compact
2. The EPs
3. The eight ILO Core Conventions on Labor Standards
4. The International Covenant on Economic, Social, and Cultural Rights
5. The International Covenant on Civil and Political Rights
6. The Children's Rights and Business Principles
7. The UN Guiding Principles on Business and Human Rights
8. The UN Convention on the Rights of the Child
9. The OECD Guidelines for Multinational Enterprises
10. UN-supported PRI
11. The Universal Declaration of Human Rights
12. The UNEP FI (SEB Corporate Sustainability Policy 2016)

Products and Services
Since 2007 SEB has committed with the World Bank to implement a fixed-income instrument and has also acted as the sole lead manager of the World Bank's inaugural SEK 2.3 billion green bond (SEB 2016 Corporate Sustainability Report 2017). SEB has been involved in the issuance of 10.8% of all green bonds globally. SEB's share in 2015 was 7.6%. In total, 40% of the total volume of green bonds has been issued on the basis of frameworks wherein SEB has served as the structural advisor (SEB 2015 Corporate Sustainability Report 2016). In 2016, SEB was the fourth-largest underwriter in volume with a market share of 4.4% equaling US$3.4 billion, and it has supported other financial sector issuers such as ABN Amro, Bank of China, BNP Paribas, DKB, Rabobank, and SBAB as a structural adviser and/or underwriter.

5.4   Learning from Experience

5.4.1   Disclosure Practices, International Engagement, and Standardization

Our analysis of reporting practices shows that standardization is yet to be realized. From a formal point of view, disclosure practices observed in the sample vary in terms of size and typology and in terms of information disclosed. With regard to forms, sustainability reporting is often integrated into annual reports (as in the case of DNB Bank) or enclosed in specific CSR documents (as in the case of BNP Paribas) (Table 5.4).

The analyzed sample reveals a wide range of reporting typologies adopted by banks and that vary from comprehensive reports—that include both financial and nonfinancial information—to specific reports and notes. The varied nature of these reporting practices can be further explained in light of countries' policies and/or in light of the adoption of international frameworks. In particular, this is the case for France where a specific regulation has been applied. In this vein, French banks must also disclose their provisions or guarantees to cover environmental risks. Thus, variability in the quality and typologies of disclosure is strictly related to countries' specific approaches to CSR and environmental issues.

Another example is represented by ING, for which the document entitled "Application of the Dutch Banking Code" provides information on corporate governance and remuneration issues, risk management procedures, and societal commitment. In addition to country-specific regulations, banks are also engaged in a series of voluntary guidelines such as those of the GRI. The adoption of the GRI standards by banks included in the sample is summarized in Table 5.5.

By excluding CA, which does not adequately disclose based on GRI guidelines Table 5.6 highlights the other banks' adherence to the standards.

Table 5.4 Documents disclosed by banks

	2016	2015	2014
Danske Bank A/S	Annual report and corporate sustainability responsibility (CSR) report	Annual report and CSR report	Annual report
ING Group	Annual report	Annual report	Annual report and sustainability annex
Crédit Agricole SA	Annual report and integrated report	Annual report and CSR report	Annual report and CSR report
BNP Paribas SA	Annual report and CSR report	Annual report and CSR report	Annual report and CSR report
DNB ASA	Integrated annual report	Annual report and Annual CSR report	Annual report and Annual CSR report
SEB	Annual report and sustainability report	Annual report and sustainability report	Annual report and sustainability report

Source: Our elaboration

Table 5.5   Adherence with GRI standards

	2016	2015	2014
Danske Bank A/S	Non-GRI[a]	GRI-G4	GRI-G4
ING Group	GRI-G4	GRI-G4	GRI-G3.1
Crédit Agricole SA	Non-GRI	Non-GRI	Non-GRI
BNP Paribas SA	Citing GRI[b]	Non-GRI	GRI-G3.1
DNB ASA	GRI-G4	GRI-G4	GRI-G4
Skandinaviska Enskilda Banken	GRI-G4	GRI-G4	GRI-G4

Source: Our elaboration from the GRI Database (http://database.globalreporting.org)
[a]Non-GRI refers to sustainability/integrated reports in which the organization discloses information on its economic, environmental, social, and governance performance but with no reference to being based on GRI guidelines or GRI standards
[b]GRI: Uses sustainability/integrated reports that make explicit reference to being based on GRI guidelines (G3, G3.1, or G4) but for which there is no GRI content index

Table 5.6   Accordance with GRI standards

	2016	2015	2014
Danske Bank A/S	Non-GRI	In accordance (core)	In accordance (core)
ING Group	In accordance (comprehensive)	In accordance (comprehensive)	A+
BNP Paribas SA	None	Non-GRI	Undeclared
DNB ASA	In accordance (core)	In accordance (core)	In accordance (core)
Skandinaviska Enskilda Banken	In accordance (core)	In accordance (core)	B+

Source: Our elaboration from GRI database (http://database.globalreporting.org)
In accordance (comprehensive) = reports contain the statement "*This report has been prepared in accordance with the GRI Standards: Comprehensive option.*"
In accordance (core) = reports contain the statement "*This report has been prepared in accordance with the GRI Standards: Core option.*"
Undeclared = no explicit "in accordance" option is declared, but the report includes a complete G4 content index

The sampled banks are also listed in sustainability indices, such as the DJSI (BNP Paribas and ING Group) and Financial Times Stock Exchange4Good (FTSE4Good) (BNP Paribas).

5.4.2   Banks' Commitments to Sustainability

In analyzing disclosed documents of the sampled banks, it is worth noting that the banks' commitments to sustainability can be summarized based on the following activities:

- Environmental considerations in terms of direct/indirect impacts and dedicated products and services
- International engagement and initiatives (e.g., UNEP FI and SDGs)

All of the sampled banks disclose information on their direct impacts on the environment. Considerable attention is dedicated—by all banks—to issues of gas emissions reduction or climate change and efforts range from the development of environmental and climate-friendly financial instruments to the adoption of special policies and goals. This is in line with international requirements (e.g., GRI) that require banks to highlight their current results that planned objectives in terms of direct impact reduction.

The risk management dimension is the most difficult to assess. While banks such as BNP Paribas and CA—forced by the French legal framework – provide many details on provisions and risk management practices, in the case of other banks information is difficult to retrieve.

With regard to the UN SDGs, only CA does not provide any information on its involvement. Table 5.7 provides an overview of the how other banks engage with the standards.

Table 5.7 shows that some objectives are prioritized by all of the banks, and that climate action is one of these.

Table 5.7   UN sustainable development goals by banks

	Danske Bank	ING	BNP Paribas	DNB	SEB
1. No poverty			✓		
2. Zero hunger			✓		
3. Good health and well-being	✓		✓		
4. Quality education	✓	✓	✓	✓	
5. Gender equality	✓		✓		
6. Clean water and sanitation		✓	✓		
7. Affordable and clean energy		✓	✓		
8. Work and economic growth	✓	✓	✓	✓	✓
9. Industry, innovation, and infrastructure		✓			✓
10. Reduced inequality			✓		
11. Sustainable cities and communities		✓	✓		
12. Responsible consumption		✓			
13. Climate action	✓	✓	✓	✓	✓
14. Life below water			✓		
15. Life on land			✓		
16. Peace, justice, and strong institutions		✓	✓		✓
17. Partnerships for the goals	✓	✓	✓		

Source: Our elaboration

5.4.3   Financial Performance and Sustainability Strategies

To explore the possibility that better financial performance may lead banks to disclose more sustainability information, Table 5.8 compares financial data to positions ranked by banks in the Top 100 Sustainability Companies ranking.

From the data and given that the Top 100 Sustainability Companies methodology (see Appendix 5.1) is based strictly on disclosed and publicly available data listed on banks' websites, it is possible to note that

1. Danske Bank moved from the tenth (in 2015) to the fourth (in 2017) position, and thus this bank improved the quality of its own disclosure practices during the period considered. Excluding the value of total assets for 2015, all of the considered variables increased in value in the same period;
2. ING Bank moved from the 45th to the 5th position in 2016/2017 and in the same period all of the considered variables decreased in value;
3. CA moved from 42th to 17th position between 2015 and 2017 and all of the considered variables decreased in value during this period except for the net income for 2016;
4. BNP Paribas moved from the 82th to the 42th position between 2015 and 2017, while the considered variables generally increased in value during this period; and
5. SEB moved from the 58th to the 46th position between 2015 and 2017, while the variable net income value decreased over the same period.

The relationship between improved financial performance and the quality of sustainability disclosure is not clear. However, it is interesting to note that if there is no clear relationship between financial performance and sustainability disclosure, the improved quality of the latter may be explained by a need to regain customer confidence. In this sense, further analysis based on statistical tools is required.

5.4.4   Sustainable Banking Products

It is interesting to note that all of the sampled banks are engaged in green bond initiatives and consequently disclose much more information despite providing other green or social products. As stressed in previous sections of this book, the development of new products and services can be viewed

Table 5.8 Financial data and sustainability companies rankings: A comparison

		2016	Δ	2015	Δ	2014	Top 100 Sustainability Companies ranking		
							2017	2016	2015
Danske Bank	Total number of employees	19.000	→	19.049	→	18.603	4	7	10
	Dividends paid	1.189.666	↑	1.084.312	↑	745.405,90			
	Total assets	468.135.575	↑	442.496.946	↑	464.016.156			
	Net income	2.668.518	→	1.763.469	↑	530.532			
ING Bank	Total number of employees	51.943	→	52.720	→	55.945	5	45	n.r.
	Dividends paid	1.345.000	→	2.200.000	↑	1.225.000			
	Total assets	843.919.000	→	1.001.992.000	↑	828.602.000			
	Net income	4.302.000	→	4.731.000	↑	2.823.000			
CA	Total number of employees	73.605	↑	71.495	→	75.396	17	n.r.	42
	Dividends paid	1.878.429	n.a	n.a.	n.a.	n.a.			
	Total assets	1.524.232.000	→	1.529.294.000	→	1.589.044.000			
	Net income	3.955.000	↑	3.971.000	↑	2.760.000			
DNB ASA	Total number of employees	11,459	→	11,840	→	12,064	34	28	46
	Dividends paid	n.a.	n.a.	n.a.	n.a.	n.a.			
	Total assets	2,653,201	↑	2,598,530	→	2,649,341			
	Net income	n.a.	n.a.	n.a.	n.a.	n.a.			
BNP Paribas	Total number of employees	192.419	↑	189.077	↑	187.903	42	35	82
	Dividends paid	0	=	0	=	0			
	Total assets	2.076.959.000	↑	1.994.193.000	→	2.077.758.000			
	Net income	8.115.000	↑	7.044.000	↑	507.000			
SEB	Total number of employees	15.300	→	15.500	→	16.000	46	41	58
	Dividends paid	n.a.	n.a.	n.a.	n.a.	n.a.			
	Total assets	267.814.938	↑	255.058.082	→	269.865.046			
	Net income	1.085.081	→	1.693.928	→	1.963.326			

Source: Our elaboration

as a market opportunity. As shown in the sections dedicated to green bonds, banks declare their efforts to fight climate change and highlight the total number of green bonds issued underwritten or arranged under a lead manager. Moreover, banks provide information on other products such as microfinance funds (as in the case of SEB) and social impact bonds (as in the case of BNP Paribas).

5.5   CONCLUSION

This chapter describes the disclosure practices of the six most sustainable banks in Europe based the notion that increased attention to sustainable banking activities from customers and stakeholders has heightened the importance of disclosure.

Banks are adopting international frameworks as a reference point to disclose their information to the public and to highlight their attention to issues such as human rights, financial crimes (e.g., antimoney laundering), and climate change. However, the adoption of well-recognized international standards—such as the GRI—does not guarantee standardization or contents of disclosure, as 50% of the sampled banks did not adopt (or cite) GRI in 2016 and among those that adopt the standards (core and comprehensive) variability in the content and level of disclosure is relevant. Moreover, comparing disclosure practices is further complicated by the presence of a large number of disclosed documents with relevant information and that integrate "core" sustainability reports. In this sense, disclosure is one of the most important instruments that banks can use to demonstrate their "sustainable approaches". However, sustainability reports are not easily accessible and are often completed by a series of other documents that do not provide an immediate overview of what banks do in terms of sustainability. Another issue that does not appear to be fully assessed in actual disclosure practices is related to the role of boards. As highlighted in previous chapters, corporate governance is a major driver toward sustainability in the banking sector. Nevertheless, information on concrete commitments to sustainability is not always available.

Finally, banks are paying more attention to the development of sustainable financial products and especially to green bonds. This confirms that banks view sustainability as a source of market opportunity.

APPENDIX 5.1: THE GLOBAL 100 SUSTAINABILITY COMPANIES

The top 100 Global 100 Sustainability Index is an international standard for evaluating corporate performance on key social and environmental issues. *Corporate Knights screens*, a Canadian magazine which manages the Global 100, analyzes nearly 5000 companies against their global industry peers to produce an annual list. The ranking is based on publicly disclosed data (e.g., financial filings and sustainability reports) and the precise ranking methodology and results of the process are fully disclosed (Global 100 Sustainability Index, 2017). The review process is described in Fig. 5.1.

From the starting universe, screening criteria are applied. The screening criteria are described in Fig. 5.2.

The shortlist obtained from the screening criteria is then analyzed from the KPIs summarized in Fig. 5.3.

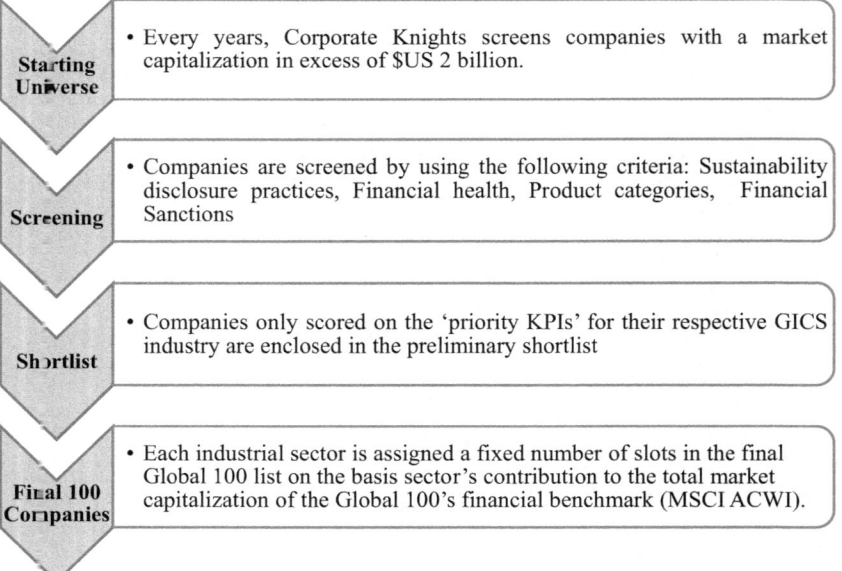

Starting Universe
• Every years, Corporate Knights screens companies with a market capitalization in excess of $US 2 billion.

Screening
• Companies are screened by using the following criteria: Sustainability disclosure practices, Financial health, Product categories, Financial Sanctions

Shortlist
• Companies only scored on the 'priority KPIs' for their respective GICS industry are enclosed in the preliminary shortlist

Final 100 Companies
• Each industrial sector is assigned a fixed number of slots in the final Global 100 list on the basis sector's contribution to the total market capitalization of the Global 100's financial benchmark (MSCI ACWI).

Fig. 5.1 The *Corporate Knight's* review process (Source: Our elaboration from Global 100 Sustainability Index (2017))

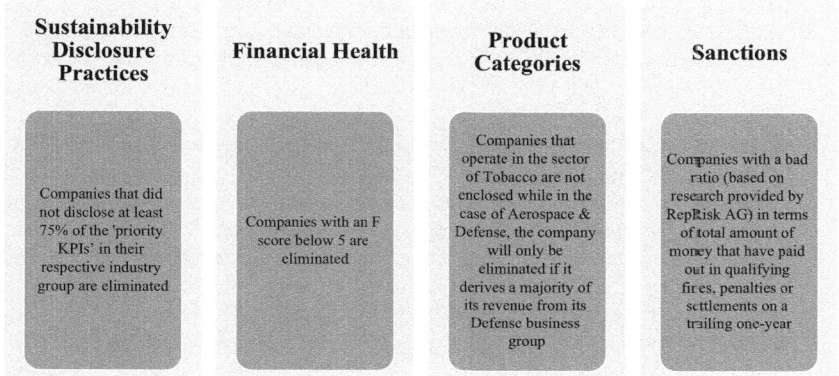

Fig. 5.2 The *Corporate Knight*'s screening process (Source: Our elaboration from Global 100 Sustainability Index (2017))

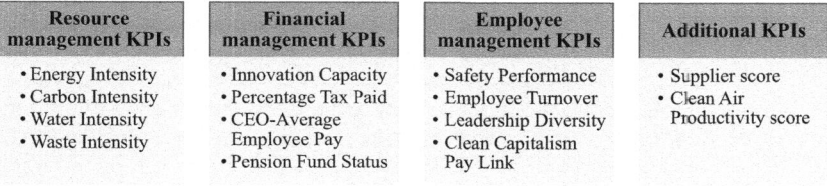

Fig. 5.3 The Global 100's KPIs (Source: Our elaboration from Global 100 Sustainability Index (2017))

NOTES

1. The OECD Guidelines for Multinational Enterprises constitute the most comprehensive international instrument on responsible business conduct (RBC). The OECD Guidelines set out principles and standards on RBC and steps that enterprises are expected to take to avoid and address involvement with adverse impacts across a range of societal concerns. For further details see OECD (2001, 2017).

2. The Climate Bonds Initiative is an international investor-focused not-for-profit organisation that works to mobilize debt capital markets for climate change solutions. It works with institutional investors, commercial actors and governments to promote investment in projects and assets necessary to support a rapid transition to a low-carbon and climate resilient economy.

The Climate Bonds Initiative also runs an International Standards and Certification Scheme for climate bonds; investor groups representing $34 trillion in assets sit on its board and some 50 organizations are involved in its development and governance. For further details see the Climate Bond Initiative website at www.climatebonds.net

3. Equator principles (EPs) are risk management frameworks for determining, assessing and managing environmental and social risk through project financing initiatives. The EPs are primarily intended to provide minimum standards for due diligence required to support responsible risk-related decisions and are conceived to ensure sustainable development in project finance. The social, ethical, and environmental policies of financial institutions that adopt this framework differ significantly from those of banks that do not adopt it (Scholtens and Dam 2007). On the role of EPs as a tool for sustainability in the financial sector, see Weber and Acheta (2014). On the relationship between EPs and bank liquidity, see Chen et al. (2017). On the relationship between the adoption of EPs and shareholder value, see Eisenbach et al. (2014).

4. The sustainable development goals (SDGs) were launched in 2015 by the United Nations. The SDGs follow the Millennium Development Goals and are a universal set of targets and indicators designed to help countries end poverty, protect the planet and ensure prosperity for all as part of a new sustainable development agenda. For further details see http://www.un.org/sustainabledevelopment/sustainable-development-goals/

5. The CDP is the global standard for the measurement and reporting of climate change information. The A List names the world's businesses leading on environmental performance. For further information see: https://www.cdp.net/

6. The Banking Environment Initiative is convened by the University of Cambridge Institute for Sustainability Leadership (CISL), which also houses the Secretariat. The BEI is a group of international banks convened by the Chief Executives of its members to identify ways to collectively direct capital towards environmentally and socially sustainable economic development. The 'Soft Commodities' Compact is a unique client-led initiative that aims to mobilize the banking industry as a whole to contribute to the transformation of soft commodity supply chains and to therefore help clients achieve zero net deforestation by 2020. It represents one of the key work streams of the BEI. Further information can be retrieved from https://www.cisl.cam.ac.uk

7. The Carbon Pricing Leadership Coalition (CPLC) was officially launched in November 2015 on the opening day of COP21, and it brings together governments, businesses and NGOs who agree and advocate that carbon pollution should be priced fairly, effectively and efficiently. For further information see https://www.carbonpricingleadership.org/

REFERENCES

Adams, C. A., & McNicholas, P. (2007). Making a difference: Sustainability reporting, accountability and organisational change. *Accounting, Auditing & Accountability Journal, 20*(3), 382–402.

Adelopo, I. (2017). Non-financial risk disclosure: The case of the UK's distressed banks. *Australasian Accounting, Business and Finance Journal, 11*(2), 23–42.

Amundi. (2016). *ESG Integration Governance, Policy & Strategy.* Montrouge.

Baxter, P., & Jack, S. (2008). Qualitative case study methodology: Study design and implementation for novice researchers. *The Qualitative Report, 13*(4), 544–559.

Bebbington, J., Higgins, C., & Frame, B. (2009). Initiating sustainable development reporting: Evidence from New Zealand. *Accounting, Auditing & Accountability Journal, 22*(4), 588–625.

Belal, A. R., Abdelsalam, O., & Nizamee, S. S. (2015). Ethical reporting in Islami Bank Bangladesh Limited (1983–2010). *Journal of Business Ethics, 129*(4), 769–784.

Bloor, M., & Wood, F. (2006). *Keywords in qualitative methods: A vocabulary of research concepts.* London: Sage.

BNP Paribas. (2012). *Registration document and annual financial report 2011.* Paris.

BNP Paribas. (2014). *Registration document and annual financial report 2013.* Paris.

BNP Paribas. (2015). *Corporate social responsibility.* Paris.

BNP Paribas. (2015). *Registration document and annual financial report 2014.* Paris.

BNP Paribas. (2016). *BNP Paribas green bond framework.* Paris.

BNP Paribas. (2016). *Registration document and annual financial report 2015.* Paris.

BNP Paribas. (2016). *The BNP Paribas group code of conduct.* Paris.

BNP Paribas. (2017). *CSR 2016 & 2017 highlights.* Paris.

BNP Paribas. (2017). *Fixed income presentation.* Paris.

BNP Paribas. (2017). *Registration document and annual financial report 2016.* Paris.

Buhr, N. (2002). A structuration view on the initiation of environmental reports. *Critical Perspectives on Accounting, 13*(1), 17–38.

Carè, R. (2017). Exploring environmental disclosure in Banks. Evidence from the euro area. *ACRN Oxford Journal of Finance and Risk Perspectives, 6*(2), 18–40.

Chen, N., Huang, H. H., & Lin, C. H. (2017). Equator principles and bank liquidity. *International Review of Economics & Finance.*

Crédit Agricole. (2016). *2015–2016 Corporate Social Responsibility. How does our responsibility contribute to our performance?.* Montrouge.

Crédit Agricole. (2015). *Registration document 2014*. Montrouge.

Crédit Agricole. (2016). *Green notes framework*. Montrouge.

Crédit Agricole. (2016). *Registration document 2015*. Montrouge.

Crédit Agricole. (2017). *Code of ethics*. Montrouge.

Crédit Agricole. (2017). *Registration document 2016*. Montrouge.

Danske Bank. (2014). *Conflict of interest policy*. Copenhagen.

Danske Bank. (2015). *Corporate responsibility 2015*. Copenhagen: UN Global Compact Communication on Progress.

Danske Bank (2016). *Corporate responsibility 2016*. Copenhagen: UN Global Compact Communication on Progress.

Danske Bank. (2016). *Corporate responsibility fact book 2016*. Copenhagen.

Danske Bank. (2016). *CSR/ESG risk assessment tool*. Copenhagen.

Danske Bank. (2016). *Diversity & inclusion policy*. Copenhagen.

Danske Bank. (2016). *Investor relations policy*. Copenhagen.

Danske Bank. (2016). *Stakeholder policy*. Copenhagen.

Danske Bank. (2017). *AML CTF and sanctions policy*. Copenhagen.

Danske Bank. (2017). *Code of conduct*. Copenhagen.

Danske Bank. (2017). *Group compliance policy*. Copenhagen.

Danske Bank. (2017). *Information management policy*. Copenhagen.

Danske Bank. (2017). *Interim report – Firts half 2017*. Copenhagen.

Danske Bank. (2017). *Remuneration policy*. Copenhagen.

Danske Bank. (2017). *Responsibility policy*. Copenhagen.

Danske Bank. (2017). *Responsible investment policy*. Copenhagen.

Danske Bank. (2017). *Stakeholder policy*. Copenaghen.

Danske Bank. (2017). *Tax policy*. Copenhagen.

Danske Bank. (2017). *Whistleblowing policy*. Copenhagen.

DN3. (2016). *CSR/ESG risk assessment tool*. Oslo.

DN3. (2016). *Group guidelines for corporate social responsibility*. Oslo.

DN3. (2017). *2016 annual report responsible investment*. Oslo.

DN3. (2017). *2016 annual report*. Oslo.

DN3. (2017). *Report on green bond proceeds*. Oslo.

Dubois, A., & Gadde, L. E. (2002). Systematic combining: An abductive approach to case research. *Journal of Business Research, 55*(7), 553–560.

Eisenbach, S., Schiereck, D., Trillig, J., & Flotow, P. (2014). Sustainable project finance, the adoption of the Equator principles and shareholder value effects. *Business Strategy and the Environment, 23*(6), 375–394.

Eisenhardt, K. M. (1989). Building theories from case study research. *Academy of management review, 14*(4), 532–550.

Gbrich, C. (2007). *Qualitative data analysis: An introduction* (1st ed.). London: Sage Publications.

Global 100 Sustainability Index. (2017). *Methodology*. Retrieved from: http://www.corporateknights.com/reports/2017-global-100/2017-global-100-methodology-14595258/

Global Reporting Initiative. (2006). *Sustainability reporting guidelines.* Amsterdam.

Guthrie, J., & Abeysekera, I. (2006). Content analysis of social, environmental reporting: What is new? *Journal of Human Resource Costing & Accounting, 10*(2), 114–126.

Hahn, R., & Lülfs, R. (2014). Legitimizing negative aspects in GRI-oriented sustainability reporting: A qualitative analysis of corporate disclosure strategies. *Journal of Business Ethics, 123*(3), 401–420.

ING. (2014). *Group sustainability annex 2014.* Amsterdam.

ING. (2014). *Group annual report.* Amsterdam.

ING. (2015). *Group annual report.* Amsterdam.

ING. (2016). *Application of the Dutch Banking Code by ING Bank N.V.* (FY 2016)

ING. (2016). *Group annual report 2015.* Amsterdam.

ING. (2016). *ING's green bond programme.* Amsterdam.

ING. (2017). *Group annual report 2016.* Amsterdam.

ING. (2017). *Environmental approach.* Amsterdam.

Islam, M. A., Jain, A., & Thomson, D. (2016). Does the global reporting initiative influence sustainability disclosures in Asia-Pacific banks? *Australasian Journal of Environmental Management, 23*(3), 298–313.

Jose, A., & Lee, S. M. (2007). Environmental reporting of global corporations: A content analysis based on website disclosures. *Journal of Business Ethics, 72*(4), 307–321.

Krippendorff, K. (2012). *Content analysis: An introduction to its methodology.* London: Sage.

Martensen, A., & Grønholdt, L. (2010). Measuring and managing brand equity: A study with focus on product and service quality in banking. *International Journal of Quality and Service Sciences, 2*(3), 300–316.

O'Dwyer, B. (2002). Managerial perceptions of corporate social disclosure: An Irish story. *Accounting, Auditing & Accountability Journal, 15*(3), 406–436.

Organization for Economic Cooperation and Development. (2001). *The OECD guidelines for multinational enterprises: Text, commentary and clarifications.* Paris: OECD.

Organization for Economic Cooperation and Development. (2017). *Responsible business conduct for institutional investors. Key considerations for due diligence under the OECD guidelines for multinational enterprises.* Paris: OECD.

Scholtens, B., & Dam, L. (2007). Banking on the equator. Are banks that adopted the equator principles different from non-adopters? *World Development, 35*(8), 1307–1328.

Seawright, J., & Gerring, J. (2008). Case selection techniques in case study research: A menu of qualitative and quantitative options. *Political Research Quarterly, 61*(2), 294–308.

SEB. (2016). *2015 corporate sustainability report*. Stockholm.

SEB. (2016). *Code of conduct*. Stockholm.

SEB. (2016). *Corporate governance report*. Stockholm.

SEB. (2016). *Corporate sustainability policy*. Stockholm.

SEB. (2017). *2016 corporate sustainability report*. Stockholm.

Spence, C. (2007). Social and environmental reporting and hegemonic discourse. *Accounting, Auditing & Accountability Journal, 20*(6), 855–882.

Vaismoradi, M., Turunen, H., & Bondas, T. (2013). Content analysis and thematic analysis: Implications for conducting a qualitative descriptive study. *Nursing & Health Sciences, 15*(3), 398–405.

Yin, R. K. (2009). *Case study research: Design and methods*. Los Angeles: Sage Publications.

Yin, R. K. (2013). *Case study research: Design and methods* (5th ed.). Thousand Oaks: Sage Publications, Inc.

CHAPTER 6

Being a Sustainable Bank: The Case of Intesa Sanpaolo

Abstract A leading banking group, such as Intesa Sanpaolo, can have a significant impact on the society and environment in which it operates. Since 2007, social and environmental issues are increasingly integrated into business strategies. This chapter explores what it means to be a sustainable bank from the internal perspective of Intesa Sanpaolo. This case highlights the role of sustainability in banks and the relevant aspects that are considered in the bank's strategy.

Keywords Sustainable banking • CSR • Social sustainability • Environmental sustainability

Cristina Laura Paltrinieri
Intesa Sanpaolo - Research & Survey
cristina.paltrinieri@intesasanpaolo.com
Rosella Carè
University Magna Graecia of Catanzaro
care@unicz.it
This chapter is the result of a collaboration between the authors: in particular, Paltrinieri contributed to Sects. 6.1, 6.2, 6.3, 6.4, 6.5, 6.6, 6.7 and 6.8 and Carè contributed to Sect. 6.9.

© The Author(s) 2018   131
R. Carè, *Sustainable Banking*,
https://doi.org/10.1007/978-3-319-73389-0_6

6.1   The Group Profile[1]

With 12.6 million customers and 4800 branches in Italy, the Intesa Sanpaolo (ISP) Group is the country's largest banking group (Fig. 6.1) and one of the top banking groups in Europe.

The Group is Italy's leading provider of financial products and services for households and businesses, particularly in banking (with a market share of more than 17% for loans and 18% for deposits), life insurance premiums (with a market share of nearly 20%), asset management (20%), pension funds (nearly 22%), and factoring (28.4%).

The Group also has a strategic presence as one of the main banking groups in Central and Eastern European, Middle Eastern, and North African countries, serving 7.6 million customers via a network of approximately 1100 branches in 11 countries (Fig. 6.2).

As of 30 September 2017, the ISP Group had total assets of €785,359 million, customer loans of €390,818 million, direct deposits from banking business of €418,407 million, and direct deposits from insurance business and technical reserves of €149,985 million. The ISP Group comprises seven business units serving different customer categories, governance areas, and central entities directly reporting to the managing director and chief executive officer (CEO).

6.2   Intesa Sanpaolo's Commitment and Values

ISP is one of the most active groups in the world in terms of economic, social, and environmental sustainability, and acts as a responsible financial intermediary to generate long-term value for the bank, its people, its customers, the community, and the environment.

ISP promotes growth based on long-term sustainable results and value creation, through a strategy built on stakeholder trust, customer and shareholder satisfaction, employees' sense of belonging, and understanding of community and local areas' needs.

Elena Flor, head of Corporate Social Responsibility (CSR) at ISP, says: *"Our way of banking has changed over time but has always remained consistent with the goal of creating a reliable financial system that is worthy of investors' trust. Transparency, soundness, careful risk management and integrity underlie our decisions and our everyday work. Service quality, staff valuing and motivation, environmental protection and a responsible resource management, as well as the numerous initiatives in favor of the community, are a concrete proof of the reliability of both our commitment and our effort to continuous improvement."*

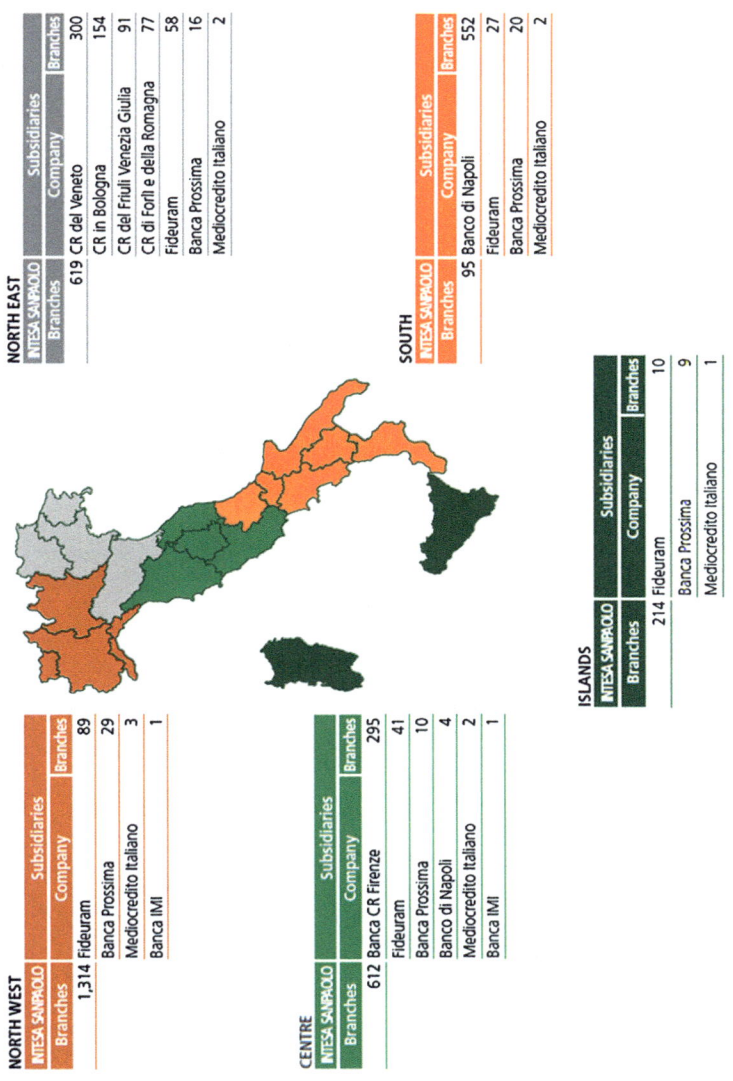

NORTH WEST

INTESA SANPAOLO Branches	Subsidiaries Company	Branches
1,314	Fideuram	89
	Banca Prossima	29
	Mediocredito Italiano	3
	Banca IMI	1

CENTRE

INTESA SANPAOLO Branches	Subsidiaries Company	Branches
612	Banca CR Firenze	295
	Fideuram	41
	Banca Prossima	10
	Banco di Napoli	4
	Mediocredito Italiano	2
	Banca IMI	1

NORTH EAST

INTESA SANPAOLO Branches	Subsidiaries Company	Branches
619	CR del Veneto	300
	CR in Bologna	154
	CR del Friuli Venezia Giulia	91
	CR di Forlì e della Romagna	77
	Fideuram	58
	Banca Prossima	16
	Mediocredito Italiano	2

SOUTH

INTESA SANPAOLO Branches	Subsidiaries Company	Branches
95	Banco di Napoli	552
	Fideuram	27
	Banca Prossima	20
	Mediocredito Italiano	2

ISLANDS

INTESA SANPAOLO Branches	Subsidiaries Company	Branches
214	Fideuram	10
	Banca Prossima	9
	Mediocredito Italiano	1

Figures as at 30 June 2017

Fig. 6.1 The Intesa Sanpaolo Italian network (Source: Intesa Sanpaolo)

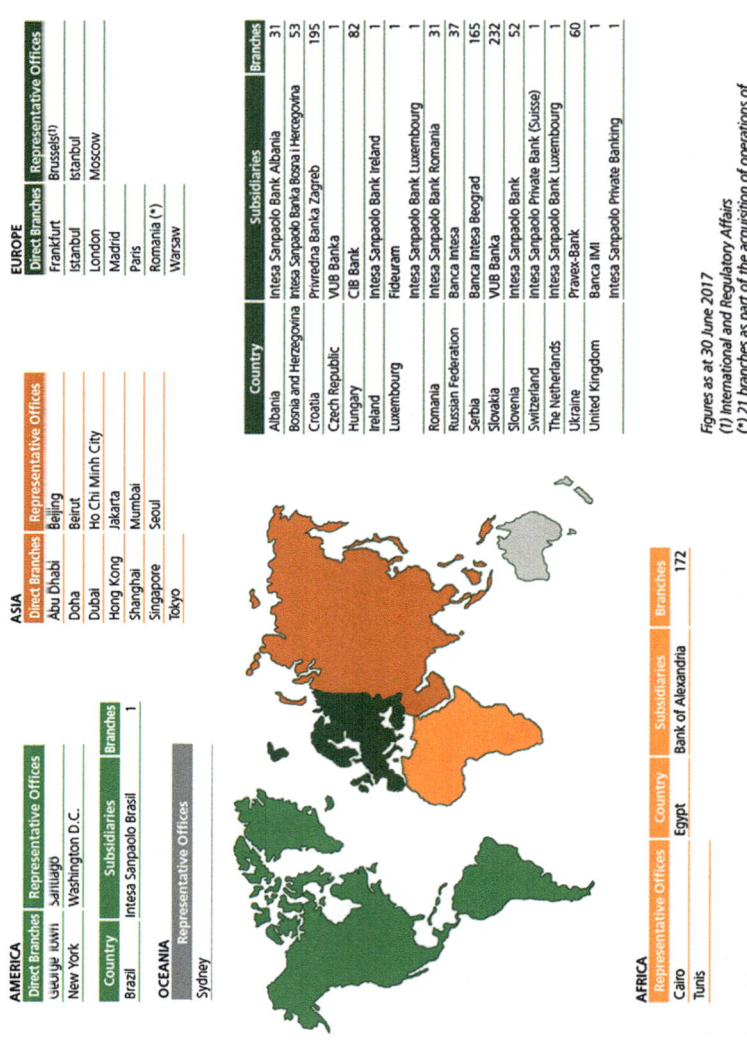

AMERICA

Direct Branches	Representative Offices
George Town	Santiago
New York	Washington D.C.

Country	Subsidiaries	Branches
Brazil	Intesa Sanpaolo Brasil	1

OCEANIA

Representative Offices
Sydney

ASIA

Direct Branches	Representative Offices
Abu Dhabi	Beijing
Doha	Beirut
Dubai	Ho Chi Minh City
Hong Kong	Jakarta
Shanghai	Mumbai
Singapore	Seoul
Tokyo	

EUROPE

Direct Branches	Representative Offices
Frankfurt	Brussels(1)
Istanbul	Istanbul
London	Moscow
Madrid	
Paris	
Romania (*)	
Warsaw	

Country	Subsidiaries	Branches
Albania	Intesa Sanpaolo Bank Albania	31
Bosnia and Herzegovina	Intesa Sanpaolo Banka Bosna i Hercegovina	53
Croatia	Privredna Banka Zagreb	195
Czech Republic	VUB Banka	1
Hungary	CIB Bank	82
Ireland	Intesa Sanpaolo Bank Ireland	1
Luxembourg	Fideuram	1
	Intesa Sanpaolo Bank Luxembourg	1
Romania	Intesa Sanpaolo Bank Romania	31
Russian Federation	Banca Intesa	37
Serbia	Banca Intesa Beograd	165
Slovakia	VUB Banka	232
Slovenia	Intesa Sanpaolo Bank	52
Switzerland	Intesa Sanpaolo Private Bank (Suisse)	1
The Netherlands	Intesa Sanpaolo Bank Luxembourg	1
Ukraine	Pravex-Bank	60
United Kingdom	Banca IMI	1
	Intesa Sanpaolo Private Banking	1

AFRICA

Representative Offices	Country	Subsidiaries	Branches
Cairo	Egypt	Bank of Alexandria	172
Tunis			

Figures as at 30 June 2017
(1) International and Regulatory Affairs
(*) 21 branches as part of the acquisition of operations of Veneto Banca

Fig. 6.2 The Intesa Sanpaolo International presence (Source: Intesa Sanpaolo)

Great importance is given to risk management and control in order to maintain a moderate risk profile, stable profits, a sound liquidity position, and a strong reputation, which are all key factors to protect both current and future profitability. Being a solid bank with growing profitability, a high capital base and a relatively low-risk profile allows ISP to positively contribute to the interests of all stakeholders and to the well-being and progress of local communities.

The Code of Ethics, adopted in 2007, is the key document that expresses the identity of ISP, its mission and values, and the principles followed in its relationships with stakeholders.

In the banking industry, where products and services are intangible, a brand's image and reputation have great importance in influencing the decisions and perceptions of consumers and stakeholders in general. Sustainability and business ethics, in turn, have a deep impact on image and reputation.

Aware of the fact that its brand is a major strategic asset, ISP is always focused on the measurement, enhancement, and protection of the image and reputation of its brand, with a view to preventing and minimizing potential negative effects.

6.3   Intesa Sanpaolo Strategic Guidelines Vis-à-Vis the Stakeholders

ISP wants to be a responsible financial intermediary that generates collective value, fully aware that innovation, the development of new products and services, and the responsibility of companies may contribute to reducing the impacts of phenomena such as climate change and the dramatic growth of social inequality on society. How does the bank want to be perceived by its stakeholders? What does it intend to be or to do for them? With regard to these two questions, ISP aims to do the following:

For Customers

- To be a real-economy bank that supports the real economy by leveraging a strong balance sheet to match healthy credit demand and managing the financial wealth of clients with care.
- To be a simple yet innovative bank, acting with a truly multichannel model.

For Shareholders

- To be a bank with sustainable profitability in which operating performance, productivity, risk profile, liquidity, and solidity/leverage are carefully balanced.
- To maintain an attractive and sustainable dividend policy, featuring a strong and increasing cash dividend distribution for the period covered by the business plan, subject to regulatory requirements: €1.2 billion paid for 2014, €2.4 billion paid for 2015, €3 billion paid for 2016, and a commitment to distribute €10 billion of cumulative cash dividends in four years (2014–2017).

For Employees

- To empower and motivate people through training, job reallocation, acknowledgment of individual merit in career development, upgrades to long-term incentives linked to productivity and results, and upgrades to company welfare mechanisms.

For Suppliers

- To set up supply systems that minimize social and environmental impacts.
- To maintain control over the supply chain, by cooperating with consumer associations and environmental and human rights organizations.

For Society and Environment

- To be a bank with a distinctive identity/reputation, committed to contributing to the growth and development of the economy and society.
- To have the CSR values deeply rooted in all business areas and staff functions, embedded in the bank's strategy, supporting social and environmental value creation for long-term economic development and respecting all stakeholders.

6.4   Corporate Social Responsibility in Intesa Sanpaolo

In ISP, the task of monitoring and coordinating the various issues related to social and environmental responsibility is entrusted to a dedicated structure, the CSR Department. It reports through the chief governance officer to the managing director and CEO and board of directors (Fig. 6.3).

The CSR Department's tasks include the following:

- Support management in the definition of CSR policies and strategies;
- update the Code of Ethics and monitor its application;
- preside over the competent structures of the dialogue and relations with the socially responsible investors;
- collaborate with other Group structures in the assessment of social and environmental risks in business development;
- provide the social and environmental reporting;

Fig. 6.3 Organizational structure of the CSR area (Source: Intesa Sanpaolo)

- preside over the dialogue with stakeholders on the issues of competence;
- set environmental guidelines by developing long-term plans of action with the competent departments and monitoring their implementation; and
- support training and communication activities on social and environmental issues.

The CSR Department reports periodically to management on the application status of the Code of Ethics, on critical elements, and on stakeholders' reports of any violation of the corporate principles and values, as well as on the consequent corrective actions envisaged.

Spotting the critical elements is made possible by periodic analyses conducted by an independent specialized consulting company to assess the consistency of corporate management processes with the values of the Code of Ethics.

The CSR Department collaborates with a network of delegates within the various departments in Italy and abroad. This Network, established in 2007, is a pivotal element of the self-responsibility model upon which the implementation of the ISP Code of Ethics is based. Its task is to share the experiences of departments where delegates operate and report any significant situation concerning social and environmental responsibility to the managers of the head office departments, the divisions, and the Group banks.

Delegates help CSR to identify the social responsibility objectives of the reference departments, manage relations with stakeholders, monitor current projects, draw up the Sustainability Report, and pinpoint and manage cases of noncompliance with the Code of Ethics.

A number of yearly public reports bear witness to the results of these continuous efforts:

- *Sustainability Report* (from 2017 *Nonfinancial Information*)—provides an account of ISP's capacity to operate consistently in keeping with its values, responding to the expectations of all the people it handles.

  Additionally, it is a management tool for monitoring progress and planning improvements, thus increasing stakeholder satisfaction.

- *Community Paper*—highlights and assesses ISP's contribution to the community and related impact.
- *Stakeholder engagement and improvement objectives*—gathers all the feedback collected through various channels from stakeholders, particularly on the Bank's activities with regard to social and environmental responsibility issues, and identifies areas for improvement.

6.5   SOCIAL SUSTAINABILITY

ISP, thanks to the traditions of the almost 250 banks that gradually merged into the Group, stands out for its strong focus on its territory and for its significant support to the communities in which it operates for their economic, environmental, and social development.

In 2016, the Bank issued loans for initiatives with a high social impact amounting to over €4.6 billion (of which €200 million was issued to the third sector and €76 million to microcredit projects), promoting financial inclusion and economic empowerment and creating new opportunities for growth.

ISP also joins, through Banca Prossima and Mediocredito Italiano, the Ministry for Economic Development, the Italian Banking Association, and CDP—the country's financial institution controlled by the Ministry, which aims to promote the companies' development—in a program to support the growth of the social economy.

The Group is also committed to the community through donations, managing temporary situations of difficulty in local areas and long-term solidarity, the sponsorship of projects with a positive impact on the community, substantial investments in art and culture, and company volunteering initiatives and programs involving all Group personnel.

In 2016, the ISP Group recorded an overall contribution to the community, measured by the London Benchmarking Group (LBG) standard,[2] amounting to over €50.3 million. The majority of this consists of cash contributions (€46.4 million), of which

- 52% consists of community investments—namely, contributions characterized by long-term plans and/or strategic partnerships and/or of sizeable amounts—which show an ever-greater strategic characterization of the Group's community activity aimed at long-term collaborations that can bring a real benefit to the community;

- 38% consists of commercial initiatives (mainly sponsorships) with community benefit, which contribute to social causes while benefiting ISP brand and business;
- 10% consists of charitable gifts, one-off or intermittent support of lesser amounts.

In terms of the scope of intervention, arts and culture are the most significant areas accounting for 58.2% of total cash contributions, followed by economic development, education and research.

Attention to art and culture is a priority element of the strategy that drives the community supporting activities of the Bank. Progetto Cultura, a strategic reference framework containing the multiyear planning of the Bank's cultural initiatives, has several objectives:

- Contributing to the country's cultural growth by sharing and making publicly available the impressive heritage of historical, artistic, architectural, editorial, and documentary assets of ISP as a result of the patronage that was historically and traditionally ensured by banks that have joined the Group;
- safeguarding and making the most of the Italian historical and artistic heritage through the restoration program *Restituzioni*, the promotion of museums and public art galleries through the systematic publication of their catalogs, and by sponsoring cultural events organized by highly renown institutions.
- planning and organizing exhibitions;
- supporting scholarships for training opportunities and research in collaboration with universities; and
- loaning of works to temporary exhibitions.

The first of the above-listed programs is centered on a network of museums, called Gallerie d'Italia, hosted in Milan, Naples, and Vicenza at some of the Bank's most impressive historical premises, which now stand as buildings of major architectural and civic importance. Gallerie d'Italia houses art collections (ranging from archaeological finds to the art of the twentieth century, approximately 20,000 works of art) and precious archives as a legacy of the banks that merged into ISP over time.

Remarkable recent examples of such activities are the Francesco Hayez exhibition (approximately 120 works presented) and the exhibition dedicated to Venetian landscape painting ("Bellotto e Canaletto. Lo stupore e la luce"), containing approximately 100 exhibited works.

6.6   Environmental Sustainability

Since 2007, the ISP Group adopted an environmental policy approved by the management board, which paid special attention to the protection of the environment. This commitment has extended to include, within the policy, not only environmental but also energy issues. The aim is to reduce the Bank's ecological footprint, to protect the ecosystem, to support research and innovation for improving energy performance and to analyze risks and climate change opportunities, in order to incorporate them into company policies.

6.6.1   *Reducing the Bank's Ecological Footprint*

Some of the most significant measures that ISP has taken concerning its own operations include:

- reducing CO_2 emissions resulting from electricity and thermal energy consumption by 13.1% in 2016 alone;
- 97% electricity consumption from renewable sources in Italy (80% at Group level); and
- 93% recycled or ecological paper on the total purchased in Italy (89% at Group level).

6.6.2   *Green Finance*

In 2016, 3.1% of ISP's total loans to business referred to environmental protection sectors, such as renewable energy, energy efficiency, and environmental services, amounting to approximately €1.7 billion, allotted as follows: project finance 47.0%, business and third sector loans 22.9%, public finance 20.3%, retail financing 8.5%, and leasing 1.3%.

Regarding retail customers, loans were disbursed for, among others, the energy efficiency renovation of property, the purchase of ecological equipment, and the installation of solar and photovoltaic panels.

In Italy, Mediocredito Italiano, ISP Group's bank that brings together medium- to long-term financing, leasing, and factoring, made an important contribution with its "tailor-made" financial solutions for businesses and public administration investing in renewable energy plants or in energy efficiency processes developed by energy-intensive or energy service companies. These loans, overseen by the Energy Desk, are preceded by project appraisals that support the Bank's credit process.

Banca Prossima, the ISP Group's bank dedicated to nonprofit organizations, continued to support third sector companies that want to invest in energy-efficient projects with solutions to save on energy costs and increase the overall sustainability of social activities. In 2016, approximately €1.2 million of funds was earmarked for projects through an operating agreement with Federesco (the National Federation of Energy Service Companies), and Banca Prossima won the "Green Globe Banking Award" in the "indirect impact" category.

Through its "Circular Economy" project, the ISP Group is seizing strategic opportunities to become an innovative and exclusive financial leader for the circular economy, redefining traditional financial tools to support the transition to a new model for economic development that is sustainable over time. As a Global Partner of the Ellen MacArthur Foundation, ISP promotes the best experience of leading international companies with Italian small and medium-sized enterprises (SMEs), creating synergies and shared value.

In June 2017, ISP was the first Italian bank to issue a €500 million green bond, which posted orders amounting to €2 billion. The proceeds were used to fund projects in the renewable energy and energy efficiency areas. The bank will publish a yearly report on the various projects.

An internal department of qualified individuals (the "Green Bond Working Group"), comprising the Treasury Department, the CSR Department, and Mediocredito Italiano, will review and approve, as appropriate, each proposed loan based on an agreed list of eligible categories and criteria.

6.6.3   Responsible Investment

ISP is aware of the positive influence that major institutional investors and banks are able to exert in the activation of sustainability dynamics among the companies they invest in or liaise with.

Eurizon Capital, the ISP Group's asset management company, embraced the Principles for Responsible Investment (PRI), geared to achieving a sustainable global financial system, born from the partnership between the United Nations Environment Programme Finance Initiative (UNEP FI) and the UN Global Compact, after having contributed to their development. In November 2015, ISP was one of the first companies to subscribe to the Italian Stewardship Principles.

In 2016, the Bank's ethical system was implemented with new benchmarks provided by Morgan Stanley Capital International (MSCI), one of the most important companies worldwide for environmental, social, and governance (ESG) research. An additional research service focused on ESG topics was also implemented by MSCI ESG.

The application of the ESG criteria resulted in the variation of the investment universe, with inclusions and exclusions of various issuers in the investment portfolios. Among the main reasons for stock inclusion ISP generally considers greenhouse gas reduction programs, biodiversity, clean tech, suppliers' involvement, and protection of minorities in the workforce. Exclusions are mainly triggered by the involvement in arms, antitrust violations, accounting frauds, and discrimination in granting credit.

To guarantee that management choices respond to the above-mentioned ethical principles, Eurizon has set up a Sustainability Committee, which is independent and autonomous with respect to the company, composed of professionals of heterogeneous extraction, with significant experience in various sectors of social responsibility concerning the management of products (bioethics, alternative energy, corporate governance, law, medicine, environment, and equal opportunity). Only one member of the Committee represents the company.

Fonditalia Ethical Investment is the socially responsible investment solution of Fideuram-ISP Private Banking, which integrates income objectives with financial sustainability and social value aspects.

It is worth noting that the Fondo pensione Gruppo Intesa Sanpaolo (ISP's pension fund) is the first in Italy to adopt an active shareholder strategy, interacting directly with a number of large companies included in the portfolio and recommending improvement measures on topics of particular interest to customers regarding social, environmental, and governance issues.

6.7   INTESA SANPAOLO'S PARTICIPATION
IN INTERNATIONAL STANDARDS AND PROGRAMS

ISP undertakes to observe the principles of sustainable development and has adhered to important international initiatives aimed at promoting dialogue among firms, international organizations and society in general and to pursue respect for the environment and human rights. The most important are as follows:

- The *Global Compact Advanced Programme* for human rights, job protection, environment, and the fight against corruption
- The *UNEP FI*
- The *Equator Principles* (voluntary international guidelines for project financing activities)
- The *Carbon Disclosure Project* (an international nonprofit organization that manages a global disclosure system on climate change for companies)
- The LBG (an internationally recognized standard for companies' reporting of community investments)

Furthermore, ISP is a member of the business communities that support the UN's sustainable development goals. The most significant projects and activities already identified refer to

- microfinance projects,
- the use of renewable sources,
- employment protection,
- training and promotion of new entrepreneurship,
- support of start-ups (tech-marketplace),
- the management of environmental emergencies, and
- the prevention of corruption.

6.8   AWARDS AND INCLUSION IN INDEXES

The Bank is included in several sustainability indexes, where selection is based not only on financial performance but also on social and environmental performance (ESG analysis).

The most relevant are the Dow Jones Sustainability Indices, whose selection is dependent on an annual assessment carried out by Robeco SAM, with a best-in-class criterion based on three aspects: economic and governance, social, and environmental. For its sustainability performances, ISP was included in the Robeco SAM Sustainability Yearbook 2017 and received the Bronze Class Sustainability Award 2017.

The strong commitment to the development of a low-carbon economy has recently been rewarded by the Carbon Disclosure Project (CDP) with the ISP's confirmation in the 2017 "Climate A List", which includes the 112 companies that reached Level A for their performance in climate change mitigation. CDP is the international nongovernmental organization (NGO) that analyzes environmental information at the request of investors representing over $100 trillion in managed funds.

ISP is also included in:

- the Financial Times Stock Exchange4Good (FTSE4Good) Global and FTSE4Good Europe, which considers only publicly available information on the three ESG areas—ESG—with assessment in 14 sectors and the use of approximately 350 indicators;
- the MSCI Global Sustainability, with assessment based on the three ESG areas, and MSCI Low Carbon, for which carbon emissions are assessed;
- the Euronext Vigeo Europe 120 and Euronext Vigeo Eurozone 120, where inclusion is based on an assessment conducted on the three ESG areas and includes an analysis of any dispute;
- the Ethibel Excellence Investment Register (Global and Europe), based on the assessment conducted by the rating agency Vigeo Sustainability on the three ESG criteria and includes the analysis of any dispute;
- the UN Global Compact 100 stock index, the 100 companies adhering to the ten principles of the UN Global Compact that stood out at a global level in terms of their attention to sustainability issues, and their performance in the financial sector;
- the Standard Ethics Italian Bank, with assessment based solely on corporate governance, and Standard Ethics Italian, based on CSR and corporate governance;
- the ECPI indexes, where the assessment is based on the analysis of public information on the three ESG areas and on the assessment of controversies;
- the Diversity and Inclusion Index (D&I—Thomson Reuters), where ISP is ranked 28th among 4000 listed companies, whose performance is measured in terms of diversity, inclusion, and professional development; and
- the STOXX© Global ESG Leaders Index, which includes companies that are leaders worldwide in terms of ESG criteria, based on ESG indicators provided by Sustainalytics.

ISP's projects in the sustainability field obtained numerous awards:

- In January 2017, the ISP was assigned the 20th position in the Global 100 ranking, drawn up by *Corporate Knights*, a Canadian magazine specializing in clean capitalism, which includes the top 100 sustainable companies in the world. It is the only Italian banking group in the ranking.
- The Group's commitment to people has been rewarded with the "Diversity & Inclusion Award 2017" and the inclusion in the EQUILEAP—Gender Equality 2017 Ranking, which includes 200 companies that stood out for their commitment to gender equality. The project "ISP Digital Learning: Portal and Smartphone App to Learn Anytime, Anywhere" was rewarded with the "Distribution and Marketing Innovation Award".
- For the attention to the environmental issues, in 2016, the Bank was included in the Newsweek Green Rankings and awarded as "Industry Carbon Leader 2016" by ET Index Research.

In November 2017, ISP was also awarded the special prize "Mecenate del XXI Secolo" (twenty-first-century patron of arts) of the Corporate Art Awards in Rome, thanks to the quality and scope of its art initiatives, which are "unparalleled in the world", the grounds of the acknowledgment said.

The Corporate Art Awards are promoted by pptArt, the first crowd-sourcing platform in the field of arts, and LUISS Business School, the private university supported by the Italian Industrialists Association. The Awards aim to identify and promote outstanding cases of patronage on an international scale.

6.9   Conclusion

The analysis of the ISP case shows that sustainability issues are a key element in the way in which the Group operates. ISP has promoted numerous initiatives for the economic and social development of the community, often centered on the founding values and the code of ethics of the Group. At the same time, ISP adopted concrete actions to fight climate change both considering its direct impact and in terms of financial products and investments. With regard to sustainability reporting, ISP shows great attention to international initiatives such as the Equator Principles, and the Group's efforts to create long-term value for all stakeholders have been recognized at the international level with its inclusion in numerous sustainability indexes.

Notes

1. Data as of November, 2017.
2. London Benchmarking Group (LBG) is an internationally recognized standard for companies reporting of community investments.

Looking Back, Looking Forward

Abstract This chapter comments on the main topics discussed in the book. In particular, the chapter highlights the main future of sustainable banking and designs a set of themes meriting further investigation from researchers in future studies.

Keywords Sustainable banking • Disclosure • Social banks

7.1 ARE WE MOVING TOWARD A PARADIGMATIC SHIFT?

The main critiques of mainstream finance have been explored in Chap. 2. Perceived as being too far from the real word and unable to understand the real market's behavior, mainstream finance has been accused of being the real cause of the 2007–2008 financial crisis. For many years, finance and ethics have been considered as dichotomic concepts. Chapter 2 shows that many authors have rejected this perspective, while others propose to relax the basic assumption of mainstream finance by proposing a paradigmatic shift toward social sciences and new epistemological approaches. Recent developments in behavioral finance and social finance literature seem to be headed in this direction. Moreover, a new academic and practitioner's movement is emerging. In this sense, is it possible to enumerate the United Nations Environment Programme Finance Initiative (UNEP FI) Manifesto for positive impact (described in Chap. 3) and the "Postcrisis

© The Author(s) 2018
R. Carè, *Sustainable Banking*,
https://doi.org/10.1007/978-3-319-73389-0_7

Finance Research Manifesto" (described in Chap. 2). Future studies in this field may be devoted to understand the real scientific maturity of these emerging practices.

7.2   SOCIAL BANKING *VERSUS* SUSTAINABLE BANKING: MAIN DIFFERENCES

Social banks have been analyzed in Chap. 2, both from a theoretical point of view and from the practical perspectives of Charity Bank and Triodos Bank (see Appendix 2.1). From a theoretical point of view, several authors highlighted that social banks are not a new phenomenon but a typical European phenomenon with many years of history. The renewed interest in social banks is essentially related to their "resilience" to financial crises, their focus on noneconomic criteria, and their delivery of financial services that have positive social, environmental, or sustainable impacts to individuals and organizations. From a practical point of view, and thus from the analysis of Triodos Bank and Charity Bank, the following main characteristics emerge:

1. Social banks focus their attention on the measurement of their impact. In this sense, both banks have developed impact measurement methodologies based on qualitative and quantitative factors.
2. Social banks provide loans only to specific categories of borrowers that generally are not considered by traditional banks.
3. Social banks have a declared social mission and operate not only considering their risk and return but also their social impact.
4. Social banks provide information on loans and banking operations in a transparent manner.

Unlike social banks, sustainable banks are traditional banks that operate by following a sustainable approach. This type of bank does not have a clear social or charity approach in their mission statement, but, on the contrary, is formed to pursue profit. Sustainable banks try to mix their risk and return considerations with impact and sustainability considerations. In particular, the sustainable approach of these kinds of banks revolves around disclosure, risk management, new products, reputational concerns, and compliance with voluntary or mandatory requirements.

From the comparison between social banks and sustainable banks, some clarifications emerge. First, social banks are by nature sustainable banks, while the opposite is not true. Sustainable banks are by nature "profit oriented banks" that pursue their sustainable aims in a strategic manner. New sustainable products, new risk management practices, and new disclosure practices confirm that these banks are trying to be sustainable but with an eye on reputation, brand image, market share, and, in general, performance.

7.3   Are NGOs and Regulators Pushing Toward Sustainable Banking?

Despite the increasing adoption of voluntary code of conducts and of voluntary disclosure practices, banks are constantly pressured to communicate their engagement in sustainability. However, to date, much information has not been disclosed, and standardization in sustainability reports is not a reality so far. This is due to the presence of different regulatory requirements in different countries. An example can be seen in Chap. 5, related to a French corporate duty of vigilance law that requires multinational French companies to establish and implement a diligence plan that should state the measures taken to identify and prevent the occurrence of human rights and environmental risks resulting from the companies' activities, the activities of companies they control and the activities of subcontractors and suppliers. At the same time, French banks have to also disclose their provisions or guarantees to cover environmental risks. Moreover, many authors, from a theoretical point of view, analyzed the relationship between sustainability disclosure and bank performance. The results in this field are not yet definitive; thus, further research may be useful.

7.4   Emerging Market Opportunities from Risk Management

As highlighted in Chap. 3, the banking sector as a whole is less concerned about its direct environmental impact than with the implications of the direct impact of their customers' activities. In this sense, banks have become more interested in appraising corporate environmental risk and performance when they lend or invest money (Lee et al. 2002). This is because, in terms of the direct impact on the environment, the banking industry is generally perceived as a "clean sector" compared with other sectors such as oil and gas or transportation (Viganò and Nicolai 2009: Bouma et al. 2017). Only recently, indirect risks—such as reputation and the responsibility related to lending activities—were duly considered (Viganò and Nicolai 2009). Moreover, in the case of underestimated environmental risk, capital can be overallocated to higher-risk activities. Thus, environmental risk analysis can support a more efficient allocation of capital for long-term sustainability. Risk management activities have the major role of protecting banks from environmental risks and related costs, but, at the same time, they may represent harmful instruments for creating new business opportunities. In particular, during the last years, new sustainable products and services have emerged. The emergence of these new products represents a way for banks to improve their offers by capturing new customers or to diversify the banks' own portfolio and consequently mitigate their risk exposure. Finally, banks actively engaged—and perceived—as sustainable or green may increase their reputation among customers, financial regulators, and the entire financial system.

7.5   Concluding Remarks

This book provides an overview of the concept of sustainable banking by moving from the relationship between ethics and finance. By questioning the essence of neoclassical finance, particularly the assumptions of profit maximization and rationality, many scholars agree on the need to reconsider the role of finance in society and the need to consider different epistemological and methodological approaches. In particular, several authors are paying attention to the need to relax the rigid assumption of traditional finance toward a more "humanistic" approach. As highlighted in the final paragraph of Chap. 2, this book does not aspire to understand if it is time for a Kuhnian revolution. However, much has been done, and some emerging topics seem to be the academic responses to the crisis of traditional finance. In particular, two main areas of research are emerging: behavioral finance and social finance. Chapter 2 focused on the second by pointing out how finance can be useful for society by giving priority to ethical and ecological choices, social utility, public interest, sustainable development, and long-term returns over short-term profit maximization.

Moreover, the analysis conducted in previous chapters—and in particular in Chap. 3—revealed that there are two major trends in the literature relating to sustainability issues in the banking industry. The first strand analyzes the relevance of sustainability/environment disclosure (Campbell and Slack 2011; Carnevale and Mazzuca 2014), and the second studies how sustainability issues are integrated into risk management models, lending practices, products, and services (Thompson and Cowton 2004; Weber et al. 2010; Weber 2012; Weber and Banks 2012; Weber et al. 2015).

For this reason, Chap. 4 explored the new banking practices that are emerging and explored in details new sustainable banking products and the issues related to sustainability disclosure. The same aspects have then been explored from a practical point of view in Chaps. 5 and 6. With regard to Chap. 5, the chapter provides a multiple case study analysis based on six European banks that are included in one of the most important sustainability ranking lists (Top 100 Sustainable Companies). From the comparison, some important aspects have emerged:

– Sustainability disclosure is influenced by the regulatory environment in which banks operate (as in the case of Dutch and French banks);
– despite the fact that banks refer to international voluntary frameworks, sustainability disclosure is far from standardization;
– risk management practices take different forms, but in every case, risk management practices are related to the need to preserve reputation and brand image; and
– all banks included in the sample provide sustainable products. In particular, all banks are active in the market of green bonds, both as issuers and as underwriters.

Chapter 6 provided an overview of Intesa Sanpaolo, from an internal point of view. In fact, Chaps. 5 and 6 have been developed to provide an overall understanding of what banks do and of what banks perceive as a sustainable engagement. The profile of a bank with a strong commitment to society and communities emerges from Chap. 6.

The attentions to environmental issues and especially to environmental risk management have increased during the last years. Many regulatory and international frameworks have been developed and have been variously applied based on many specific factors, such as size or legal context. Finally, by incorporating sustainability principles into corporate strategy funding decisions and product/service definition processes, banks can be influential in supporting and promoting environmentally and/or socially responsible projects and enterprises and thus may have a central role in promoting sustainable development.

References

Bouma, J. J., Jeucken, M., & Klinkers, L. (Eds.). (2017). *Sustainable banking: The greening of finance*. New York: Routledge.

Campbell, D., & Slack, R. (2011). Environmental disclosure and environmental risk: Sceptical attitudes of UK sell-side bank analysts. *The British Accounting Review, 43*(1), 54–64.

Carnevale, C., & Mazzuca, M. (2014). Sustainability report and bank valuation: Evidence from European stock markets. *Business Ethics: A European Review, 23*(1), 69–90.

Lee, B. W., Jung, S. T., & Chun, Y. O. (2002). Environmental accounting in Korea: Cases and policy recommendations. In M. Bennett & J. J. Bouma (Eds.), *Environmental management accounting: Informational and institutional developments. Eco-efficiency in industry and science* (Vol. 9, pp. 175–186). Dordrecht: Springer.

Thompson, P., & Cowton, C. J. (2004). Bringing the environment into bank lending: Implications for environmental reporting. *The British Accounting Review, 36*(2), 197–218.

Viganò, F., & Nicolai, D. (2009). CSR in the European banking sector: Evidence from a survey. In *Corporate social responsibility in Europe: Rhetoric and realities* (pp. 95–108). Cheltenham: Edward Elgar Publishing.

Weber, O. (2012). Environmental credit risk management in banks and financial service institutions. *Business Strategy and the Environment, 21*(4), 248–263.

Weber, O., & Banks, Y. (2012). Corporate sustainability assessment in financing the extractive sector. *Journal of Sustainable Finance & Investment, 2*(1), 64–81.

Weber, O., Scholz, R. W., & Michalik, G. (2010). Incorporating sustainability criteria into credit risk management. *Business Strategy and the Environment, 19*(1), 39–50.

Weber, O., Hoque, A., & Ayub Islam, M. (2015). Incorporating environmental criteria into credit risk management in Bangladeshi banks. *Journal of Sustainable Finance & Investment, 5*(1–2), 1–15.

Index[1]

---

[1] Note: Page numbers followed by 'n' refer to notes.

© The Author(s) 2018
R. Carè, *Sustainable Banking,*
https://doi.org/10.1007/978-3-319-73389-0

Printed by Printforce, the Netherlands